D0982980

THE HUMAN FUTURES SERIES

Barry N. Schwartz and Robert L. Disch,
General Editors

ANNA K. FRANCOEUR has had a varied career, teaching social studies and mathematics in high schools and comparative civilizations on the college level. With a Master's degree in history from New York University, she is presently a cost accountant with Rowe International, a member of the select Groves Conference on Marriage and the Family, mother of two daughters, and coauthor of *Hot and Cool Sex: Cultures in Conflict* (1974).

ROBERT T. FRANCOEUR is the author of several books on evolution, theology, ethics, and biology, most notably *Utopian Motherhood: New Trends in Human Reproduction; Eve's New Rib: Twenty Faces of Sex, Marriage, and Family*; and, with his wife, coauthor of *Hot and Cool Sex: Cultures in Conflict*. A consultant to the American Medical Association on reproductive technology, father of two daughters, lecturer, his primary work is professor of human sexuality and embryology at Fairleigh Dickinson University.

the future
of sexual relations

EDITED BY *Robert T. and Anna K. Francoeur*

PRENTICE-HALL, INC.  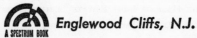 *Englewood Cliffs, N.J.*

Library of Congress Cataloging in Publication Data

FRANCOEUR, ROBERT T   comp.
    The future of sexual relations.

    (The Human futures series) (A Spectrum Book)
    Bibliography: p.
    1. Sex customs—Addresses, essays, lectures.
2. Marriage—Addresses, essays, lectures. 3. Sex
(Psychology) I. Francoeur, Anna K., joint comp.
II. Title.
HQ21.F76   301.41   74-19201
ISBN 0-13-345918-7
ISBN 0-13-345900-4 (pbk.)

10 9 8 7 6 5 4 3 2 1

PRENTICE-HALL INTERNATIONAL, INC. (London)

PRENTICE-HALL OF AUSTRALIA PTY. LTD. (Sydney)

PRENTICE-HALL OF CANADA LTD. (Toronto)

PRENTICE-HALL OF INDIA PRIVATE LIMITED (New Delhi)

PRENTICE-HALL OF JAPAN, INC. (Tokyo)

contents

foreword & preface

Predicting the future of sexual relations, like predicting the future of anything that involves volatile human populations and numerous unweighted variables, is a highly speculative venture unless firmly rooted in present realities and identifiable tendencies. Hence this collection, edited and written by Robert and Anna Francoeur, is rightly concerned with delineating those influences that are already affecting our psychosexual lives and will unquestionably continue to do so in the future. They and their contributors wisely avoid telling us what things will be like in the year 2,000; nor do they give us science fiction scenarios in place of reasoned analysis. Rather they address themselves to an unflinching examination of the psychological consequences and social problems developing out of those changes that are already upon us.

There are, of course, no easy ways to side-step these problems, although it is very likely—for reasons discussed below—that many will try. As Dr. Francoeur points out in the opening essay of the book, the sheer impact of the scientific and technological changes that directly affect human sexuality, reproduction, and social relationships unavoidably touches many other aspects of personal life and society at large. Such readily available sexual technologies as the pill, genetic screening, sperm banks, artificial insemination, safe abortion, vasectomy, transexual surgery, and predetermination of fetal sex have directly altered the lives of many individuals and changed the ways in which many others think about sexuality and reproduction. And there are a host of developing technologies discussed in both the first essay and throughout the book that when perfected will influence the future of sexual relations and further invade the once private domains of conception, gestation, and parenthood.

For obvious reasons, the ultimate impact of these and other developments on the biological and social future of humanity remains beyond the pale. It is only necessary to speculate about the social consequences that would follow if a scientist were to announce the discovery of an economical method of indefinitely prolonging life to realize that, at such a juncture, human history would literally begin anew. Instantly the traditional definitions of what it means to be human would be called into question. But what else would follow must be left to the imaginative visions of artists and writers.

Ironically, though, while scientific discoveries and technological innovations can alter human history in ways that are well beyond rational comprehension, they are also—to some extent at least—within reach of governmental and social controls. Many scientists have refused to work on projects they consider dangerous or inhuman, or whose results they don't want placed in the hands of political or business leaders. At present, congressional committees are considering legislation that would restrict experimentation with human fetuses and embryos and, in concert with the scientific and business establishments, are trying to find ways to assess the side effects of all new technologies before they are widely adopted.

It is true that the history of the uses and abuses of Western science and technology does not lead to optimism about the possibilities of restraining either scientific research or technological applications. Nevertheless, the cessation of atmospheric atomic testing by some nations and the refusal of Congress to fund the SST do suggest that restraint can be displayed in the face of conspicuous threats to health or survival. Nor would controls necessarily inhibit the advancement of pure science. As Paul Goodman pointed out some time ago, we can give *carte blanche* to scientific research so long as we are scrupulously attentive to the potential abuses of the technologies that are made possible by scientific discovery.

But if there are at least a few precedents to suggest the possibility of bringing controls to bear on science and technology, there is no way to halt the psychosexual changes described in this collection. Such recent developments as the widespread use of sexual and reproductive technologies, the increasing practice and acceptance of bisexuality, the revolt of women against male-dictated identities, the appearance of many different forms of child rearing (including gay and lesbian parenthood), and the growing recognition of the androgynous nature of the human animal are all part of an apparently irreversible trend toward a radical restructuring of sexual relationships. All of these (and other) changes are now in motion and seem utterly irreversible and beyond either social or political control. The results are in: Sexual relationships and their social structures will be increasingly based on the awareness discussed in this collection.

This is not to suggest that the ideas, proposals, and even the specific topics dealt with by the contributors will not meet with resistance, hostility, and derision from people in all walks of life. The past, as twentieth-century history endlessly reveals, and as revolutionary history itself points up, persists tenaciously into the present. What will *not* be easily relinquished is the security derived from the folklore and custom that has traditionally defined sexuality. Nor will the new forms of behavior that flow from changing concepts of sexuality be readily embraced, or even tolerated, by much of society. As the Francoeurs and others have pointed out, all of the dislocations that result from the changes in sexual relationships will be exacerbated by the rapid pace of change in all areas of life. With so little time to adjust to developments affecting these deeply personal and highly taboo areas, we can expect mounting social tensions and perhaps reactionary movements aimed at a return to allegedly simpler days. Certainly, the issues discussed in this book threaten those vestiges of the past that will be most reluctantly abandoned.

It is possible to argue that the pressures being generated by the psychosocial changes described in chapters two through four pose a greater threat to social stability than do the more spectacular but potentially controllable developments from the biology labs. As the upheavals of the 1960s revealed, the United States (and other Western countries) is divided in ways that both include and go beyond the obvious differences of class, ethnicity, religion, and politics. We can reasonably anticipate that a further fragmentation of American life will be brought on by the challenges to tradition posed by the new forms of sexual relationship discussed in these chapters.

Already there are ferocious debates underway about abortion; divorce; civil rights for women, children, and transexuals; birth control for minors; and lesbian and gay parenthood—to name a few of the more publicized issues.

If these problems are to be resolved with a minimum of social distress, educators will have to bring the issues before their students, the media will have to inform the public at large, and politicians and the courts will have to find the courage to accomodate in law the rights of people who choose unconventional life-styles compatible with their needs. In short, the amelioration of social conflict generated by these issues demands a degree of institutional responsiveness that has not been particularly characteristic of institutions in the past.

The value of the Francoeurs' book, then, is that it confronts the questions openly, honestly, and optimistically. It supplies the reader with a wealth of valuable factual and historical information as well as with perceptive, humanistic analyses concerning the future of sexual relations. Taken together the contributors see in these transformations the evolution of a fuller humanity free from the deadening stereotypes and social patterns that fail to meet the requirements of people living in the late twentieth century. Like Camus' Sisyphus, the book embraces its difficult task with vitality, commitment, and love.

ROBERT DISCH

The essays gathered in this volume focus on the possible and probable paths humans may pursue in the decades ahead in the ongoing evolution of sexual relationships and the institutions which support these relations. Each of the contributors deals with the future of sexual relations, often focusing on a single aspect such as parenthood, marital values, or male/female images. But always this focus is situated within a broader social or historical context.

Two pivotal themes run through all the essays. The first theme reminds us that human behavior, like all animal behavior, is a response or adaptation of individuals and their societies to a particular environment. The way we relate as men and women today, the patterns of our marriages and family life, are direct responses to the environment we live in. For survival and happiness we have to find a way to be comfortable with the contraceptive pill, the economic independence of women, liberalized divorce and abortion laws, and countless other environmental factors. The second theme reminds us that over the centuries we have constantly created new environments because our curiosity leads us to invent new and more sophisticated tool-making arts. New technologies create new environments, and new environments force us to adapt our behavior, our values, and our institutions.

The essays in this collection deal with the wide variety of twentieth-century technologies and their roles in creating the radically new social environment we are experiencing. They also explore in depth the psychological, moral, and social impact of this new environment as it molds our relationships as sexual persons today and in the decades ahead. The questions dealt with are simple to state, but the answers offered are provocative and challenging in their insight for the future of human relationships:

- What new technologies have come into our social environment? Can we foresee their overall impact on marriage and the family?
- What kind of changes are twentieth-century technologies leading us to in our interpersonal values and expectations?
- How have our religious traditions molded our sexual attitudes and values in the past, and what role are they likely to play in the future?
- How are our images of male and female changing?
- How are we likely to behave and relate as men and women in the future?
- What will be our values, attitudes, and expectations in the realm of interpersonal and sexual relationships?
- How will we meet our need for human community and companionship?
- What will be the role of sexuality and its function in a zero-growth population?
- What will be the most functional pattern of pair-bonding in the future: serial polygamy based on patriarchal values and divorce and remarriage, or some sort of "open marriage" based on a new set of values?
- Is traditional parenthood a dying vocation?
- Is the nuclear family dying, and if so, what will replace it in our society?
- Will men and women accept the new genetic and reproductive technologies with the likelihood of the designed human and licensed parenthood?
- How can men cope with the sexually liberated woman? How can they avoid "the new impotence?"
- What will our new family norms be like? What about the single-parent family and the transexual family?
- Does our future lie in a tribal "Cool Sex" androgynous culture? What might this mean for our potential as persons, our relationships as sexual beings?

This collection, then, presents a broad but detailed picture of the past, present, and future of human sexual relations. Its purpose is not to answer questions, but rather to provoke the thought and discussion needed to answer the questions we all are facing in our relationships today and tomorrow.

ROBERT T. AND ANNA K. FRANCOEUR

our technologies

In the opening essay, an experimental embryologist sets the stage for our exploration by summarizing the many faces of our reproductive technologies. Dr. Francoeur begins his summary by tying together three seemingly discrete change factors in our world: the exponential growth of science and medicine, the socioeconomic emergence of women in our society, and mass global communications. With these three factors as a backdrop, the present state of reproductive technologies, artificial insemination, frozen sperm, embryo transplants, artificial wombs, asexual reproduction, prenatal monitoring and manipulation, transexual operations, frozen embryos, and behavior control, all take on new meaning as elements in our radically new ecosystem. This opening essay also provides a prognosis for these reproductive technologies in the next decade or two and a summary of basic environmental factors such as life expectancy and infant mortality which make today's world so different from the one that married and single men and women knew only fifty or a hundred years ago.

Chapter 1

the technologies of man-made sex

Robert T. Francoeur

There are some unique characteristics apparent in the revolution we are witnessing today in human sexual behavior. In other social revolutions triggered by man's new technologies it was difficult, if not impossible, to diagnose the patient's condition while the fever of change still afflicted him as an individual and as a member of society. This is not the situation with our sexual revolution. For various reasons the basic character and trends in the sexual revolution are already evident, even to the casual observer outside the deliberate and scientific disciplines of sociology, family relations, anthropology, and psychology.

One unique characteristic of the sexual revolution is the swiftness of its impact on the average citizen in the Western world and in many developing nations. Previous technological revolutions have created their own cultures and modified human behavioral patterns along with the structure of society, the relations of men and women, and the pattern of the family. The discovery of fire and agriculture, the invention of wheels, gunpowder, steam and internal combustion engines, automobiles, nuclear power, television, and space travel— each of these technologies has triggered revolutions in man's vision and handling of his world. Adaptation to these new technologies naturally reverberates throughout the whole fabric of human culture to modify our patterns of family life and basic human relations. Sometimes these changes were hardly noticed, at other times they were more apparent and drastic. The fragmentation of the sexes and the emergence of sexual roles that came with the advent of agriculture and

"The Technologies of Man-Made Sex" by Robert T. Francoeur. This article appears for the first time in this book.

urbanization over ten thousand years ago modified the relations of men and women almost imperceptibly because the shift to urban life was spread over many generations and centuries. In some areas this shift is just now touching the last remnants of nomadic and tribal cultures. A more recent innovation, the automobile, has had a more devastating impact because it practically destroyed the Victorian American extended family and created the new reality of the so-called nuclear family of mobile post–World War I America. This shift took only four or five decades to sweep a continent.

But agriculture, urbanization, automobiles, television, and industrialization are technologies whose practical results, applications and impact are *parapersonal*. They are out there, so to speak, and do not really impinge directly on each person in a culture or society. They are tools *we use*, extensions of our senses and muscles, but only *indirectly* do we incorporate them into our personalities or allow them to affect our thinking and behavior. They mold the periphery of our lives. Their impact consequently has been at best the creation of a gradual change, at worst the birth of a painfully rapid upheaval.

The technologies of sex discussed in this anthology are quite different. The new technologies of reproduction, contraception, sexual modification, and genetic designing crash into the very intimate nature of the human, exploding our concepts of male and female. They throw into chaos our deepest images of ourselves as sexual persons, our most treasured and seemingly stable images of male-female relations, marriage, parenthood, and family. *These technologies affect every man and woman alive today*. They are creating a revolution which amounts to *a period of apocalyptic discontinuity*, probably the first discontinuity of such magnitude to occur since humankind appeared two million years ago.

The reason for this radical discontinuity, I believe, can be traced to more than just the fact that reproductive and genetic technologies now threaten our basic images of man and woman as sexual persons who relate in set structures of marriage and family. The discontinuity is also due to the interplay of three basic factors which may seem discrete and unrelated, but which are in reality closely interwoven.

First is the extraordinarily rapid acceleration in the advance of science and medicine. Ninety percent of all the scientists in human history are living today. An equal portion of important scientific and medical discoveries has occurred in the last century or so.

If our recent discoveries of the contraceptive pill, the intrauterine devices, the minipills, vasectomy and intervas valves, sperm banks, and other contraceptive hardware had occurred a thousand years ago, their advent would have been spread over centuries. Lazaro Spallanzani, one of the earliest experimenters in reproductive technology, successfully inseminated some frogs and dogs artificially in 1776 and 1780. Thirty years passed before the technique was applied to a woman in England, and another 150 years passed before this technique became a fairly common mode of human reproduction. If artificial insemination were to be discovered today it would be known and practiced around the world within five or ten years. This is exactly what happened with the technology of the contraceptive pill. And with ninety percent of the scientists alive and working today, it is small wonder that the pace of scientific and medical research today has entered what the statistician would call an exponential or geometric growth phase. Within a decade or two our technology has plunged us into the midst of *man-made sex:* artificial insemination, frozen sperm and egg banks for humans, embryo transplants, surrogate mothers, genetic selection and modifications, predetermination of fetal sex, conception control, legalized abortion, and transexual operation are already in use. And tomorrow holds the probabilities of artificial wombs, asexual forms of human reproduction, and genetic engineering. Most of these new technologies have developed within this century!

The second social factor or vector is the equalization of the sexes. This socioeconomic revolution is epitomized but hardly encompassed in the phrase *women's liberation.* As Teilhard de Chardin repeatedly stated, this century is witnessing a critical threshold in the hominization of the human race: the emergence of women as human beings and as independent persons socially and economically. Throughout most of human history the brute animal strength and aggression of the human male has denied true humanity to women, constantly defining them as incomplete creatures who depend on the male for their identity. As dependent persons, women have traditionally drawn their identity from their roles as wives and mothers. Now, because of women's accelerating economic independence, this "relative" existence is changing. With women no longer chained to their roles as domestic support systems for the male, our whole society changes. This is why the so-called sexual revolution is a revolution that affects our whole social fabric and culture.

Finally, these two vectors—devastating enough if taken alone or together—combine with our transistorized, near-instantaneous communications network. As McLuhan and others have pointed out, we are fast becoming a global tribe in which communications satellites, transistorized battery-powered radios, and television sets reach the most isolated cultures. Today, if a group of doctors and scientists are trying to solve the problem of childless couples in which the wife's oviducts are blocked, all it takes is an interview with one of these patients on the evening television news and millions are soon made aware of the potential of artificial inovulation or embryo transplantation. *Look* magazine picks it up for a cover story, *Family Circle* and *Woman's Day* peddle the message in the supermarket, television talk shows carry it to night owls and the housewife at her morning coffee break.

In my own files I have several dozen inquiries from women around the country who feel that embryo transplants might provide a satisfactory solution to their own childless condition. In several cases, female neighbors or relatives have volunteered to carry the child. Attitudes are changing, and it could well be that surrogate motherhood will become a socially acceptable option, an alternate way of parenthood in the decades ahead.

One final illustration will conclude our look at the impact of television and the printed word on our changing images of male and female, marriage, and parenthood. The case that I have chosen is not uncommon and will likely become more common in the years ahead. Paul Grossman, a fifty-three-year-old music teacher from Plainfield, New Jersey, his wife of some twenty years, Ruth, and their three daughters went through a crisis in the spring of 1971. At the age of fifty, Paul finally reached the breaking point in coping with an affliction he had suffered with since his earliest memories. Born with a perfectly normal male anatomy and genetic constitution, he unfortunately did not have a matching male psychosexual identity, probably due to a perinatal hormone imbalance that allowed female imprinting of the brain. When the joy of his fiftieth birthday party dissolved, Paul broke down and discussed his condition and decision with his wife and teenage daughters. Within weeks Paul had arranged with Dr. Harry Benjamin's clinic in New York City for a transexual operation. After the operation, *Paula* returned to her teaching position where the principal allowed her to continue provided she wore her customary male garb. But the contract for the coming school year created more serious problems and resulted in her being denied a contract despite her tenured position. The case is now in the courts, and eventually may reach the United States Supreme Court for decision on job discrimination on the basis of sex.

Again, however, the mass media comes into play as a molder of public opinion and an agent for rapidly changing our traditional concepts. Thousands of transexual operations have been performed in the United States since the first one in 1931. Paula's case is unique only in that she took a public stand and remained very visible. Her case has become internationally known as a result of her many appearances on television, newspaper interviews, and public lectures around the country. More recently, Jan Morris, a renowned British journalist, has told the story of her transition from male to female status in the best seller *Conundrum,* thus adding to the public impact of this medical procedure.

TODAY'S TECHNOLOGIES

>—*The exponential growth of science, technology, and medicine*
>—*The liberation of women as persons*
>—*The near-instantaneous global network of television, communications satellites, and the printed word*

These are the complicating factors in our revolution. But what about the actual raw materials, the technological advances in human reproduction that directly modify and revolutionize our traditional images of male and female, parenthood, and the relationships of men and women?

To answer this question let us look first at what is already available, already a part of our world:

Artificial insemination, which allows conception and parenthood without genital intercourse, was first accomplished in 1776. In 1799, an English woman gave birth to the first human conceived with what then became known as "ethereal copulation." When British scientists successfully froze semen without damage in 1949, artificial insemination became a very practical reproductive technology for all animals. With domesticated animals, artificial insemination with frozen semen is the common mode of reproduction for cattle, turkeys, and sheep. On the human level, common estimates suggest that somewhere around one percent of all the children born in the United States today are conceived by artificial insemination.

Frozen human sperm banks had their commercial start in October 1971 when a fourteen-year-old private sperm bank in Minnesota decided to open a public service branch in New York City. In the months that followed, human sperm banks began to appear in many locations around the United States. Eighteen such facilities were functioning by the end of 1972, with four more scheduled to open in early 1973.

Embryo transplantation (artificial inovulation) became a reality for domesticated animals in the early 1950s. The first successful *in vitro* fertilization of a human egg to be followed by transfer to a surrogate mother was done by Landrum B. Shettles at Columbia Presbyterian Hospital in New York City in late 1970. Similar experiments with women have been attempted in England and Australia. As of mid-1973 no human fetus had yet gone full term after transplantation, but this is an almost inevitable outcome of these experiments. It may already be a reality in Dr. Edwards' laboratory at Cambridge, where a two-year silence on embryo transplant experiments has followed some initially promising announcements.

Artificial wombs are under active research in a dozen laboratories around the world in attempts to understand the nature of pregnancy and birth. At the National Institute of Heart and Lung Diseases in Bethesda, Maryland a premature human fetus was maintained in an artificial womb for several days. Experiments with lamb fetuses have been far more successful and promising. The Russians claimed in the late 1960s to have maintained a human fetus for six months before terminating the gestation.

Asexual reproduction, parthenogenesis (virgin birth) and cloning from a single parent made their appearance in 1896 when French scientists produced virgin-born sea urchins, and in 1952 when Briggs and King first transplanted an adult nucleus into enucleated frog eggs. Parthenogenetic rabbits came in 1939 with the work of John Rock, and virgin-born mice in 1970 through the efforts of some Polish scientists.

Predetermination of fetal sex made a major step towards reality when Landrum B. Shettles combined several well-known facts about sperm morphology and physiology into a six-point "recipe" for boys or girls which he claims is eighty-five to ninety percent accurate. His "recipe" appeared in a cover story in *Look* magazine in 1970 and then in a full-length book entitled: *Your Baby's Sex: Now You Can Choose.*

Transexual operations began in 1930 when a Dutch artist underwent a complete plastic surgery transformation from male to female anatomy. In its first three years of operation the Johns Hopkins Gender Identification Clinic received inquiries from over 1500 persons interested in a transexual operation. Doctors at Stanford University estimate that probably two thousand such operations were performed in the United States in the last four years.

Uterine transplants have been partially successful in work with rhesus monkeys, but not yet with humans as of 1974. In Brazil, a woman had a normal pregnancy after becoming the recipient of an *ovary transplant.* One *transplant of a vagina* has been reported in Greece, where a forty-five-year-old widow allowed the transplantation of her vagina to her daughter who was born with none.

Embryo fusions, resulting in what geneticists call allophenic offspring, have been produced by Beatrice Mintz working at the Institute for Cancer Research in Philadelphia. Very young mouse embryos can be taken from their mother's oviducts after normal mating and conception. Even when two or three embryos are produced in two or three mothers of different genetic strains—black, white, mottled, hooded—they can be fused together into a single embryo and transferred to the womb of a surrogate mother, where they develop and are born normally. Such embryos have four or even six genetic parents of *both* sexes.

Minimenstruation has been developed out of abortion technologies so that women can use suction machines to remove the menstrual endometrium and thereby reduce the normal several days of menstruation to a brief fifteen minutes.

Frozen embryos are another reality of reproductive technology. Dr. Wittingham has successfully frozen young mouse embryos in liquid nitrogen for upwards of eight days. When they were thawed, Wittingham was able to transplant them to surrogate mothers, in whose wombs they developed normally. After birth, these same exfrozen mice were indistinguishable from their nonfrozen siblings.

Animal/plant hybrids are in their earliest stages of development, with tissue-culture hybridizing of chloroplasts from African violets and spinach with mouse cells, and the hybridizing of chromosome material from viral and mouse sources with living humans. Several pioneering experiments are now under way to determine whether viral hereditary material can be hybridized with the defective chromosomal material of children with arginemia, a serious type of mental retardation due to a missing genetic unit.

New species and sexes of animals are another product of our reproductive technology that is just beginning. James Danielli reported his success in 1971 in combining the nucleus of one species of amoeba with the cell membrane of a second species and the cytoplasm of a third species. The result was a totally new species of amoeba with hereditary information from all three species. Emil Witschi has created a new kind of female frog. *Xenopus laevis* females normally have ZW sex-determining chromosomes and the males ZZ. Z and W are used for the sex chromosomes instead of X and Y when the female determines the offspring's sex by producing two kinds of sperm. By experimentally reversing the sex of developing tadpoles and then mating the products, Witschi produced a normal female with WW chromosomes.

This brief inventory covers the main areas of our genetic and reproductive technologies as they stand in early 1974.

MALE/FEMALE ECOSYSTEMS

Important as our reproductive and contraceptive technologies are in molding our social structures, values, attitudes, and behavioral patterns, *they do not stand alone*. The technologies are part of a total ecosystem in which we and our children live. Our present images of what it means to be male and female, of marriage and parenthood— our attitudes, values, and expectations—have been molded and modified by countless factors in our environment other than the technological. These I want to touch on, however briefly, because they also are vital in understanding and appreciating the future of human sexuality, marriage patterns, and parenthood.

Our traditional male/female images and patriarchal form of monogamy evolved when mankind enjoyed a relatively short *life expectancy*. A million years ago the average human lived eighteen years. Two thousand years ago, average life expectancy was up to twenty-two years, and in the middle ages, up to thirty-three years. Today, our life expectancies are in the low and middle seventies for Americans. In some developing nations life expectancies have doubled in one or two generations. What does this do to marriage, the family, and our images and expectations for ourselves? What if our life expectancy goes over a hundred years?

Infant mortality rates have dropped rapidly with the advances of modern medicine and the discovery of antibiotics. So also has the size of our families. In colonial America the average family had ten to twenty children, with twenty to thirty not uncommon. Today, the average American family is down to 2.01 children, with many couples having no children at all.

Mobility has affected our images and expectations and values. The average American moves once every five years and fourteen times in his lifetime.

The average work week has dropped within two centuries from six days, twelve to fourteen hours per day, to a common five-day, forty-hour work week. A growing trend is evident towards four-day, ten-hour-a-day weeks, or even three-day, twelve-hour-a-day weeks. *Retirement,* once unknown, is now down to sixty years, pushing into the fifties, and projected within a couple of decades to be down into the forties. Leisure affects us very much in what we value and expect out of life.

In 1940, seventeen percent of all American wives worked outside the home. Today nearly half of all American wives are working.

As the economic basis and function of the monogamous family continue to fade in the posttechnological age, so does the link between marriage and parenthood. One out of every six minors in the United States is in the custody of a single parent. Half the children born in the District of Columbia in 1973 were born out-of-wedlock. The number of single men and women under thirty-five has doubled in ten years to fifty-six percent for men and forty-five percent for women. Single persons, homosexuals and lesbian couples can now legally adopt or raise children in many states.

In the past couple of centuries better nutrition and other factors have lowered the average age of puberty for both men and women from around twenty to the very early teens. Simultaneously, social factors, including the need for more education, have led to the postponement of marriage into the early twenties, five or six years later than it occurred a few centuries ago. The sexually mature single person is a relatively new phenomenon in human society.

Finally, our divorce rate has moved from one divorce for every seven marriages in 1920 to more than 3.8 divorces for every ten marriages in 1972.

When all our present and emerging technologies with their psychological impact are combined with the broader environmental factors just listed, one can easily see why we are in a state of apocalyptic discontinuity which is already producing radical changes in the relationships of men and women.

images and models
of sex

A vital aspect of being human is the propensity, perhaps even the instinctual need, for men and women to create myths and models which then guide their behavior and reduce the constant decision-making to a manageable dimension.

In this section, an embryologist, a theologian, an educator-publisher, a futurist specializing in communications and a historian analyze traditional images of male and female and the institution of marriage and indicate how these images are already changing. They also explore the values, attitudes, and expectations that seem to be gathering around a new image of what it means to be a sexual person, male or female, in a world where technology has made sexual intercourse an experience distinct from procreation.

Marshall McLuhan, the author of *Understanding Media: the Extensions of Man* and a half dozen other controversial books, has been variously labeled "the most important thinker since Newton, Darwin, Freud, Einstein and Pavlov," a prophet, a fake social scientist, a poet, a shoddy scholar, and an erudite pop philosopher. If nothing else, he is a provocateur and catalyst for creative thinking. His collaborator in the essay that follows is George B. Leonard, author of *The Man and Woman Thing and Other Provocations,* a vice-president of the Esalen Institute of San Francisco and for seventeen years a senior editor for *Look* magazine. Joining their insights, McLuhan and Leonard sketch a fascinating, penetrating history of sex and its evolution to SEX. They suggest a new social myth—which later essayists in this volume will expand on—the myth of traditional Hot Sex and our emerging tribal Cool Sex attitudes, values, and expectations.

George B. Leonard has had some second thoughts on the social myth of Hot and Cool Sex which he and McLuhan first suggested in 1967. Coming a few years later, these after-thoughts suggest some very positive elements in our social, global evolution towards a cool-sex culture. Leonard asks some catalytic questions about the dangers inherent in reducing human sexuality to genital interlocking, the relationship between sensuality and sexuality, and the causal connection between hot-sex mentalities and various paraphilias such as pornography, prostitution, and violent sex.

Taking off from the seminal model of Hot and Cool Sex suggested by McLuhan and Leonard, Anna K. and Robert T. Francoeur build a detailed picture of these two mythic but real images. They draw their details from elements in our lives today, from current movies and novels. Hot Sex, it soon becomes evident, is part and parcel of the typological pattern of thought which sees male and female in terms of unchanging, eternal, sexist stereotypes, whereas the Cool-Sex images are typically less easy to define and constantly evolving with the unique experiences of individual persons. In this framework, the Cool-Sex model detailed here is an abstraction whose realities are found only in the infinite incarnations of everyday people.

The Hot- and Cool-Sex models are then set in comparison with another set of social models, that of the closed and open marriage analyzed by Nena and George O'Neill in their 1972 best-seller *Open Marriage*. Four lists are suggested which clearly delineate the attitudes, values, and expectations of Hot and Cool Sex, Closed and Open Marriages.

Theologian Rosemary Radford Reuther finds in the sexual images and models of the past a real optimism for the future of man and woman. Picking up the theme of woman's emergence in society as a person, she suggests that our hope for the sexual human requires a new image of woman, no longer necessarily a domestic image and certainly no longer a patriarchal image in which women are defined in terms of their relation to men. Sex, separated by technology from reproduction, must now be personalized. Sexuality, Reuther argues, "signifies the potential for ecstasy in interpersonal relations." But she also highlights the problem in this regard: historically, men have been far more afraid of communications between men and women than they have been of sex itself. The male-dominated society has handled this fear of communications and of sex by betraying the human potential of sexuality. Historically they have sublimated its ecstatic powers and reduced their sexuality to genital sex, whether as an ascetic or a libertine experience. The solution is to *personalize* human sexuality.

Chapter 2

the future of sex

Marshall McLuhan and George B. Leonard

"Well, it finally happened," Michael Murphy of California's Esalen Institute recently said. "A young person came up to talk with me, and I couldn't tell if this person was a man or a woman. Now, I've seen plenty of young people of both sexes dressed in slacks, sweater and long hair, but I'd always been able to find *some* sexually distinguishing clue. This time there was *no way for me to tell*. I admit it shook me up. I didn't know exactly how to relate. I felt it would take a new kind of relating, no matter if it were a boy *or* girl."

The episode is extreme, but it points to a strong trend. In today's most technologically advanced societies, especially urban Britain and America, members of the younger generation are making it clear—in dress and music, deeds and words—just how unequivocally they reject their elders' sexual world. It is tempting to treat the extremes as fads; perhaps many of them are. But beneath the external symptoms, deep transforming forces are at work.

Sex as we now think of it may soon be dead. Sexual concepts, ideals and practices already are being altered almost beyond recognition. Marriage and the family are shifting into new dimensions. What it will mean to be boy or girl, man or woman, husband or wife, male or female may come as one of the great surprises the future holds for us.

We study the future the better to understand a present that will not stand still for inspection. Today, corporations, foundations and governments are asking a new breed of experts called "futurists" to tell them how things are going to be. These futurists tend to limit their predictions to things rather than people. Their imaginations and their computers fight future wars, knit future systems of economics, transportation and communication, build future cities of fantastic cast. Into these wars, systems and cities, they place people just like us—and thereby falsify all their predictions. By default rather than design, most futurists assume that "human nature" will hold firm. They ignore the fact that technological change has always struck human life right at the heart, changing people just as it changes things.

This may be especially true of sex. A history of mankind in terms of sexual practices would make wildly variegated reading. Many ancient civilizations, for example, encouraged varying degrees of incest, and the Ptolemies, successors to Alexander the Great, practiced marriage between brother and sister for some three hundred years with no obvious ill effect. Modern anthropologists have brought back stories of present-day primitive tribes whose sex customs confound our traditional notion that there is only one "natural" pattern of relationship between the sexes.

In early man, just as in most of the higher mammals, males and females lived rather similar lives, with little specialization except where childbearing and childrearing were concerned. Life for every member of a primitive hunting tribe was integral, all-involving; there could be no feminist movement, nor any special class of homosexuals or prostitutes. But when mankind turned from hunting to farming, and then to creating cities, empires, pyramids and temples, men and women were split apart in ways that went far beyond biology. Many men became specialists—kings, workers, merchants, warriors, farmers, scribes—in the increasingly complex social machine. Most women fell heir to less specialized, but separate, domestic tasks.

With the coming of writing, it was the manly virtues that were recorded and extolled. As Charles W. Ferguson points out in *The Male Attitude*, men have kept the records of the race, which may explain why history is a chronicle of war, conquest, politics, hot competition and abstract reasoning. "What survives in the broad account of the days before the modern era," Ferguson writes, "is a picture of a humankind full of hostility and inevitable hate." (LOOK researchers were surprised to find that, until relatively recent times, female births and deaths often were not even recorded.) Ancient writers exaggerated the biological as well as the social differences between the sexes, with the female coming off very badly indeed.

The Romans invented the word *sexus*, probably deriving it from the Latin verb *secare*, to cut or sever. And that is exactly what civilization has done to man and woman. The cutting apart of the sexes rarely has been more drastic than in the industrial age of Europe and America, the period that was presaged by the invention of printing around 1460, and that is now changing into something new right before our eyes.

Throughout the Middle Ages, there had been less separateness between men and women. Privacy, for example, was unwished. Houses had no hallways; bedrooms served as passageways and sleeping places for children, relatives and visitors, along with married couples. Under such circumstances, the sexual act merged easily with the rest of life. Language now considered intimate or vulgar was part of ordinary conversation. Childhood did not exist as a separate category. At about age seven, children simply moved into the grown-up world; paintings of that day depict the young as scaled-down adults, even to the matter of clothing.

After printing, however, human life became increasingly visual and compartmentalized. Architecture took up the idea of visual enclosure, with private rooms connected by hallways. It was only when this happened that childhood separated out from the rest of life. At the same time, sexual activity went underground. Hidden and mysterious, it receded into a realm apart from ordinary existence, becoming more and more fraught with a special intensity, a vague anxiety. Indecency, pornography and obscenity came into being as a result of specialist stress on separate parts of the body. By the time of Queen Victoria, the split between sex and the proper life was complete. Any wedding night, after a five- to ten-year engagement, was likely to be a trauma.

Freud flushed sex up out of the underground, but he, like his contemporaries, saw it as an explosive, a possible threat to whatever held civilization together. In his time—and even up to the present— the forces of life seemed constantly at odds with one another; since the Renaissance, it has seemed necessary to pen them up in separate compartments. The industrial age built more than its share of these boxes. It split class from class, job from job, profession from profession, work from play; divorced the self from the reality and joy of the present moment; fragmented the senses from the emotions, from the intellect; and, perhaps most importantly of all, created highly specialized and standardized males and females.

The ideal male of the industrial age was "all man." He was aggressive, competitive, logical. This man of action was also an apostle of the abstract. And he feared to show much emotion. The ideal woman, for her part, was emotional, intuitive, guilefully practical, submissive. Maleness and femaleness were separate territories; man and woman shared only a tiny plot of common humanity. The wonder is that the two could get together long enough to continue the race.

When sex—under the influence of Freud, factories, the automobile and world wars—came out into the open to become SEX, a peculiar thing happened: People were *supposed* to be free and frequent with their sexual activity. Women were *supposed* to turn from Victorian propriety to passionate responsiveness. And yet the basic ideals of maleness and femaleness continued unchanged. It was like a revolution without popular support: a lot of slogans, shouting and confusion, but not much revolution.

The only real attempt at change up until the present turned out to be abortive. Women of feminist persuasion, viewing the action and the power over there in the arena of aggressiveness, specialization and hot competition, tried to take on the attributes of maleness. How ironical! They may have been heading in the wrong direction. When the Victorian novelist George Meredith wrote, "I expect that Woman will be the last thing civilized by Man," he was unknowingly describing her fitness for the *post*-civilized Electric Age. Where the old technology split people and the world apart, demanded human fragmentation, the emerging technology is putting Humpty Dumpty back together again. It is most doubtful, in the new age, that the rigidly "male" qualities will be of much use. In fact, there may well be little need for standardized males *or* females.

Trying to define a new sexuality in the industrial period, D. H. Lawrence placed his characters against a backdrop of factories, mines, smokestacks. His most successful sexual hero (in *Lady Chatterley's Lover*) was a gamekeeper; he may be viewed as the closest Lawrence could get to the primitive hunter. In a sense, the man of the future will be a hunter, an adventurer, a researcher—not a cog in a social machine. The coming age, linked by all-involving, instantaneous, responsive, electronic communication, may seem more "tribal" than "industrial." The whole business of sex may become again, as in the tribal state, play—freer, *but less important.*

When survey-takers "prove" that there is no sexual revolution among our young people by showing that the frequency of sexual intercourse has not greatly increased, they are missing the point completely. Indeed, the frequency of intercourse may decrease in the future *because of* a real revolution in attitudes toward, feelings about and uses of sex, especially concerning the roles of male and female. What are those young men with long, flowing hair really saying? In what may seem a ludicrous overstatement, they are sending a clear message to all who will listen: "We are no longer afraid to display what *you* may call 'feminine.' We are willing to reveal that we have feelings, weaknesses, tenderness—that we are human. And, by the way, we just may be ridiculing all of those uptight movie males with cropped hair and unflinching eyes. We're betting they can't touch our girls." Indeed, the long-haired boys' appeal is not esthetic, but sexual; not private, but corporate.

Bear in mind that the Beatles' dazzling early success, long before their remarkable musicianship came clear, was conferred upon them by millions of young *females* who were transported by those pageboy hairdos and those sensitive faces. And the Beatles were not the first in a modern lineage of girl-movers. A younger, slenderer, tenderer Frank Sinatra, and then a hip-swiveling Elvis Presley, had reduced earlier sub-generations to squeals and moans. It takes a particularly obstinate blindness not to realize that an ability to free emotions, and not a fragmented "all-maleness," provides today's most compelling erotic appeal.

We might also confess that our reading of the new teen-age "conformity" of dress and hairdo fails to consider the social ritualism of these forms. They express the new desire for depth involvement in social life rather than egotistic eccentricity.

The trend (perhaps without the exaggerated hair style) seems likely to continue. The all-sensory, all-pervasive total environment of the future may be no place for the narrow-gauge, specialized male. Emotional range and psychic mobility may be valued. Heightened intuition may be required. The breed of hombre generally portrayed by John Wayne is already an anachronism. "Be a man!" the hombre bellows, and the more perceptive of our young laugh.

And if the narrow-gauge male is not laughed out of existence, he may, literally, *die* out. Specialized, competitive man is particularly susceptible to the maladies of the involuntary muscle, nervous and vascular systems. A U.S. male's life expectancy now is seven years less than a female's. Figures on earlier times are impossible to verify, but one thing is sure: the gap has never been greater. Men who operate inside the boxes of fragmented civilization—whether bus driver, pro-duction-line worker or professional specialist—die off at an alarming rate from the heart and gut diseases. Figures for the peptic ulcer are particularly revealing: deaths for white men are four times that for white women in the U.S. But the female death rate, as women have started pushing into the man's world, has been rising. And what about today's younger generation, those under 25? Here are the children of TV and science fiction, the pioneers of the Electric Age, the first hu-mans to sample, even briefly and incompletely, the less fragmented, less competitive, more involving future. What of these tentatively re-tribalized young men? We may predict that their ulcer rate will de-cline.

No surprise. In the most isolated primitive tribes, those whose members still operate as free-roving hunters, digestive disorders are practically unknown and the usual civilized heart troubles are rare. Significantly, these people make little distinction between the ideal qualities of male and female. As the noted British anthropologist Geoffrey Gorer writes concerning the peace-loving Pygmies of Africa, the Arapesh of New Guinea and the Lepchas of Sikkim: "Men and women have different primary sexual characteristics—a source of endless merriment as well as more concrete satisfactions—and some different skills and aptitudes. No child, however, grows up with the injunctions, 'All real men do . . .' or 'No proper woman does . . . ,' so that there is no confusion of sexual identity: no cases of sexual inversion have been reported among them. The model for the growing child is one of concrete performance and frank enjoyment, not of metaphysical, symbolic achievements or of ordeals to be surmounted. They do not have heroes or martyrs to emulate or cowards or traitors to despise; . . . a happy, hard-working and productive life is within the reach of all."

It would seem that "being a man" in the usual, aggressive Western sense is, if nothing else, unhealthy. To live an ordinary peacetime life in the U.S.—as a recent Army study of the "nervous secretions" of combat soldiers in Vietnam shows—is as bad or worse for your gut, heart and nervous system as facing enemy bullets. But the present fragmented civilization seems on its way out, and what "being a man" means could swiftly change.

Extremes create opposite extremes. The specialized, narrow-gauge male of the industrial age produced—in ideal, at least—the specialized woman. The age stressed the visual over the other senses; the fast development of photography, and then movies, helped pull femaleness up from the context of life, of actuality, and make it something special, intense, "hot."

Grotesque and distorted extremes tend to pop out just at the end of any era, a good example being the recent rash of blown-up photographic nudes. The foldout playmate in *Playboy* Magazine—she of outsize breast and buttocks, pictured in sharp detail—signals the death throes of a departing age. Already, she is beginning to appear quaint, not sexy. She might still be possible for a while in a wide-screen, color movie (another hot medium). But try to imagine her, in that same artificial pose, on the intimate, involving, "cool" television set in your living room.

Don't throw away your *Playboy* foldouts, however. Sooner than it may seem possible, those playmate-size nudes may become fashionable as collectors' items, having the same old-timey quality for future generations that cigar-store Indians and Victorian cartoons have for us. This is not to say that nudity is on its way out. On the contrary, it will most likely increase in the neo-tribal future. But it will merge into the context of ordinary living, becoming not so much lurid and sexy as natural and sensuous.

Already, new "sex symbols" poke fun at the super female. Notable among them is the boyish and gentle young model known as Twiggy. Sophia Loren, for example, is to Twiggy as a Rubens painting is to an X ray. And what does an X ray of a woman reveal? Not a realistic picture, but a deep, involving image. Not a specialized female, but *a human being*.

It is toward a common humanity that both sexes now tend. As artificial, socially-imposed distinctions disappear, the unalterable essentials of maleness and femaleness may assume their rightful importance and delight. The lusty Gallic salute, *Vive la différence!*, rings truer about biology than about mores, mannerisms and dress. Even fashion speaks. "Glamour" was a form of armor, designed to insulate, to separate. The new styles, male and female, invite dialogue.

While both sexes will probably change, most men will have farther to go than most women in adjusting to the new life. In an unspecialized world of computers and all-enveloping communications, sensitive intuition and openness will win more prizes, if you will, than unfeeling simplistic logic. Right now, it is impossible to guess how many companies are being held together by intuitive and sensitive executive secretaries. Fortunate is the enterprise that has a womanly woman (not a brittle, feminist dame) as a high-level officer. Many forward-looking corporations, especially in the aerospace industry, already are engaged in sensitivity-training sessions for their male executives. The behavior encouraged in these sessions would make a John Wayne character wince: Manly males learn how to reveal their emotions, to become sensitive to others, to weep openly if that is what they feel like doing—all this in the pursuit of higher profits. Sensitivity *works*. The new technology—complex, interrelated, responsive—demands it.

The demands for new male and female ideals and actions are all around us, changing people in many a subtle and unsuspected way. But there is one specific product of modern technology, the contraceptive pill, that can blow the old boundaries sky high. It makes it possible for sexual woman to act like sexual man. Just as the Bomb instantly wipes out all the separating boundaries essential to conventional war, the Pill erases the old sexual boundaries in a flash. The Pill makes woman a Bomb. She creates a new kind of fragmentation, separating sexual intercourse from procreation. She also explodes old barriers between the sexes, bringing them closer together. Watch for traditions to fall.

Romantic Love seems a likely victim. As a specialty, romance was an invention of the late Middle Ages, a triumph of highly individualistic enterprise. It requires separation, unfulfillment. The chase is everything—the man aflame, the maiden coy. Sexual consummation bursts the balloon of yearning. As in the romantic movies, the significant embrace can hardly be imagined without "The End" printed over it. Indeed, what we have called sex in recent decades may be viewed as the lag end of Romantic Love.

As a way of selecting a spouse, romance ("In all the world, you are the only girl for me") never worked very well. Back in the 18th century, Boswell may have felt some shock at Dr. Johnson's answer to his question: "Pray, Sir, do you not suppose there are fifty women in the world, with any one of whom a man may be as happy, as with any one woman in particular?" Johnson replied: "Aye, fifty thousand." The future may well agree with Dr. Johnson. It is difficult to play the coy maiden on a daily diet of contraceptive pills. And the appeal of computer dating suggests that young people are seeking out a wide and quite practical range of qualities in their mates—not just romance or high-intensity sex appeal. Here, in fact, may be the electronic counterpart of arranged marriage.

The great mystics have always perceived Romantic Love as somehow defective, as a double ego that selfishly ignores other people. Today's youngsters have a different way of putting it: "Our parents' generation is hung up about sex."

As romantic love fades, so may sexual privacy. Already, young people shock their elders by casually conversing on matters previously considered top secret. And the hippies, those brash pioneers of new life patterns, have reverted—boys and girls together, along with a few little children—to the communal living of the Middle Ages or the primitive tribe. It is not uncommon to find a goodly mixture of them sleeping in one room. Readers who envisage wild orgies just don't get the picture. Most of the hippies are *not* hung up on sex. To them, sex is merely one of many sensory experiences. It is available when desired —therefore perhaps not so desperately pursued.

Today, sex is returning to the adult world just as childhood is once again becoming enmeshed in grown-up matters. The dream girl or dream guy is becoming as odd an idea as the dream house in a world of integral urban design. Sex is becoming secondary to the young. At the same rate that it becomes accessible, it is cooling down. A couple of teen-agers like Romeo and Juliet would now have some of their most dramatic moments deciding on the kind of education they want for their children, plus a second career for Romeo in middle age.

In future generations, it seems most likely that sex will merge with the rest of life, that it will settle down and take its place within a whole spectrum of experiences. You might not think so, what with the outpouring of sexed-up novels and plays since World War II. But these, like the slickly pictured playmates, bring to mind the death rattle of an era. When a novelist like Norman Mailer contends that man is boxed-in by civilized constraints, he is quite right. But when he goes on to say that the free human spirit can now assert itself mostly through sex and violence, he is being merely Victorian.

The more that modern writers present sexual activity as a separate, highly defined, "hot" aspect of life, the more they hasten the death of SEX. Most "literary" novelists have not yet discovered the present, much less glimpsed the future; which is one reason why so many of the brighter college students have turned to anti-novels and, in spite of its questionable literary reputation, science fiction. Robert Heinlein's *Stranger in a Strange Land,* a popular underground book, tells of an attempt to set up Martian, rather than the usual human, relationships here on earth. In these relationships, what we term sex is communal and multisensual. There is no sharp, artificial distinction between male and female roles. Sex blends with other activities that might be called mystical. And there is even the need for a new word (Heinlein calls it "growing closer") for this demi-erotic mode of relating. Many young people see something of their own aspirations in the Heinlein book and others similar to it. Norman O. Brown (*Life Against Death, Love's Body*) strikes an equally sympathetic response with his thesis that civilized man has even fragmented his physical person. According to Brown, many people can feel sexual pleasure only in the sex organs themselves; the rich sensory universe of the rest of the body has been deadened.

Just as the Electric Age, with its multitudinous communication aids, is extending the human nervous system *outside* the body, it is also creating a new desire for exploration inside the self. This inner trip seeks ways to awaken *all* the senses, to find long-lost human capacities, to discover turn-ons beyond the narrowly sexual. One instance of this new drive for depth involvement is the growing national interest in Oriental religion and philosophy; another, riskier, one is increasing use of LSD and marijuana among young people. These drugs, the experimentalists claim, very quickly "blow your mind," which is to say, they knock out the old partitions within the self, allowing new connections to be made. Some theorists also say that the new rock music with psychedelic light effects can aid the inner traveler.

Serious researchers are looking for means of accomplishing even more without the use of drugs. In several centers throughout the U.S., they are working out techniques for awakening the body and senses, especially those other than the purely visual, and for helping people achieve the unusual psychic states described, for example, in the literature of mysticism. The future will likely demonstrate that *every* human being has capacities for pleasure and fulfillment beyond sex that the present barely hints at.

In this rich context, those reports on the death of the American family may turn out to have been premature. Actually, the family may be moving into a Golden Age. With so much experiment possible, marriage may come later in life than ever before. Future family units may not be separated from each other in little capsules, but may join together in loosely organized "tribes." As it is now, the capsular family often has nowhere to turn for advice and encouragement when in need, except to professional counselors or organizations. The informal tribe of the future can provide a sounding board and a source of support for each of its families, far more responsive and more loving than any professional helper.

With marriage coming later in life, it may also become a more serious matter—perhaps as serious as divorce. Some couples may even wish to write up a legally binding separation agreement (to be revised when their financial and parental situation changes) as a precondition to marriage. Thus, in a sense, marriage becomes "divorce." With all this unpleasant business anticipated and accomplished even before the nuptial vows are spoken, divorce becomes far easier—and probably far less likely. In any case, the divorce rate will probably fall.

Marriage—firmly and willfully welded, centered on creative parenthood—may become the future's most stable institution. The old, largely discredited "togetherness" was based on stereotyped concepts of each family member's role. The new family, integral and deeply involving, may provide the ideal unit for personal discovery, for experiment in the seemingly infinite possibilities of being human. Each new child can provide a new set of perceptions for all the family. Each develops rapidly, urges change in parents and other children alike. It is possible that the family of the future may find its stability in constant change, in the encouragement of what is unique in each of its members; that marriage, freed from the compulsions and restrictions surrounding high-intensity SEX, can become far more *sensual*, that is to say, more integral.

What about homosexuality and prostitution? Lifelong, specialized sexual inversion has baffled many researchers. But may it not be viewed simply as a response to sexual overspecialization? Just as men in our society are far more specialized than women, so male homosexuality is far more prevalent. To "be a man" in the narrow sense has often proven difficult and dehumanizing. In certain stressful and ambiguous family situations, some young men have not been able to pull it off. So they flip-flop over to the coin's reverse side, the mirror image of hyper-maleness—even more specialized, even more limiting.

If a new, less specialized maleness emerges, it is possible that the need to turn to specialized homosexuality will decrease. There is a striking absence of it among the communal-living young people of today.

As for prostitution, if it is the oldest profession (or, if you will, service industry), it is also one of the most ancient specialties—an early consequence of the creation of man-in-the-mass. Armies, merchant fleets, work forces: Men without women demanded Woman, or at least one aspect of her. So long as men are massed and shipped away from home, this female specialist will likely follow. But, like homosexuality, prostitution may also be looked upon as a response to a certain kind of hyper-femininity. When men, as in the Victorian Age and long after, require sexually-inhibited wives, they create an equal and opposite demand for sexually-uninhibited partners-for-pay. As the first requirement fades, so does the second. Already, call girls are becoming game for the aging. The whole notion seems somewhat ridiculous to the young.

Indeed, the future may well wonder why there has been so much fuss about sex over all these years. Sex may well be regaining some of its traditional cool. It is still a three-letter word, despite the efforts of its four-letter relatives to hot it up. This is not to say the future will be sexless. Far from it, generations yet to come may very well find *all of life* far more erotic than now seems possible.

Those who try to puzzle out any *single* sexual way for the next age will probably find their efforts in vain. Rather, it seems, the future holds out infinite variety, diversity. The search for a new sexuality is, after all, a search for a new selfhood, a new way of relating. This search already is well under way. What it turns up will surprise us all.

why we need a new sexuality

George B. Leonard

Every few months another survey taker comes along to prove there's really no sexual revolution among our young people, because the frequency of sexual intercourse hasn't greatly increased. These researchers are missing the point completely. Back in 1967, Marshall McLuhan and I wrote in LOOK that the frequency of intercourse may actually decrease in the future *"because of a real revolution in attitudes toward, feelings about and uses of sex."*

The survey takers' misconception makes a good starting point for any discussion of sexuality, since it shows exactly what's wrong with this whole area in our time and our culture. Most people, especially those of the older generation, still think of "sex" or "sexiness" in terms of nudity, genitals, breasts, number ("how many times?"), pinups and dirty jokes. They see "male" and "female" as entirely separate and opposite. They find the whole matter fraught with excitement and peril, circumscribed by taboos and guilt.

The taboos unquestionably were useful prior to modern contraception and hygiene. The highly specialized, limiting roles of male and female were probably appropriate to those earlier times when human individuals had to serve as specialized components of hard-striving, underpopulated societies. Today, these same attitudes threaten the social order, heighten the chance of violence and war, increase population pressures and needlessly restrict human pleasure and fulfillment.

Sex actually touches far more of our lives than we generally think. Because of this, sex in the narrow sense can and should become

"Why We Need a New Sexuality" by George B. Leonard. From *Look* (January 13, 1970), 5. Reprinted by permission of the author.

less "important" and certainly less fraught. The erotic impulses flow throughout complex circuits involving both brain and glands. These impulses, though concentrated in the familiar sexual zones, can be felt all over the body, and can affect every aspect of sensing and thinking. The same neural-hormonal forces that cause an erection can make the sky look bluer, a song ring clearer. Sex involves not just coitus but birth, child-rearing, family patterns, uses of affection and personal role in the world. Those censorious people who think they are protecting us from sex are just wringing the joys out of living by pressing sexuality into a dark corner—thus making it far more dangerous.

We might start making sex safe and joyful simply by renouncing all censorship. This means just what it says: Sexual intercourse and birth could be shown on network television and in family magazines. Nothing would be hidden. No need for "X" or "R" ratings for films. As it is, the censors have the age limits backwards. We must surely feel compassion sometimes for older people subjected to revelations that in their youth would have seemed to shake the foundations of the soul. Little children, until directed by word or example to think dirty, find nothing more unusual about the way a man and a woman mate than about how a tree grows or an airplane flies. The ending of all sex censorship might set off a period of adjustment, marked by a temporary increase in the sniggering portrayal of sex that currently corrupts art and life. But a totally free marketplace would give good practice a chance to drive out bad. In a very few years, preoccupation with hyped-up, "hot" sex would very likely begin to fade. Such has been the case in Denmark, where pornography for grown-ups has been legalized.

The awful silence surrounding sex in most American families builds tensions and perpetuates dangerous misconceptions. Many American parents are still so ignorant or hung-up about the subject that they want school lecturers to teach their children the facts of life. But school as it is probably won't help very much. If the traditional classroom can make things as exciting as poetry and mathematics dreaded by most students, what might it not do to sex?

We need a new sexuality; we also need a new sensuality. A society that considers most good feelings immoral and bad feelings moral perpetuates the ultimate human heresy: an insult, if you will, to God and His works. A man cut off from bodily pleasures uses sex compulsively, a spasm of release from his prison. He uses work compulsively, a narcotic to dull the pain of deprivation. Compulsive work and compulsive reproduction are exactly what we don't need in the Seventies. We need a world where people can trust their good feelings, where members of the same sex can touch and caress without fear of homosexuality, where members of the opposite sex can touch and caress without fear of seductiveness. Sensory-awareness pioneer Bernard Gunther proposes that if every person in the world gave and received a loving, half-hour massage every day, there would be no war.

Until very recently, sex in our culture has tended to become more and more specialized—by partner (spouse), part of body (genitals), "position" (male dominant), time (night) and place (bedroom). Every specialization is limiting, but the most limiting and dangerous of all is the one that artificially splits man from woman, trapping each in a rigid "role." "Be a man," often means, "turn off your feelings, wreak your will upon others and act always out of impersonal rationality." "Be a woman," on the other hand, means, "stay soft and emotional, be submissive, not smart, and act always out of intuition." Unfortunately, this sharp specialization doesn't even allow men to become good rationalists or women good emotionalists; each side, lacking the other, is crippled.

Our tragic adventure in Vietnam may be traced to outmoded ideals of "manliness" as well as to considerations of international strategy. (The strategic reasoning never made sense; the military assurances were obviously wrong.) By the very phrases they use ("pride," "cut and run"), the old men who are willing for young men to keep dying on the other side of the world reveal clearly that they see the war as a test of their manliness. Their "manly" upbringing deprived them of emotions, so they are unable to feel the suffering they cause. And they're just "rational" enough to discover ideologies worth more than other people's "mere biological survival."

The world has become too small and explosive for the narrow-gauge male. We need men who can feel deeply. We need women who can show their intelligence. We need full human beings, proud of their biological differences but unwilling to become puppets marked "male" and "female."

Ethnologists have been reminding us lately of our animal natures. (It takes a pretty disembodied culture to need reminding.) Perhaps it's true that our distant past as hunters required fast breeding, with lasting pair-bonding to assure care for our slow-maturing young. Now, these tendencies work against us, creating overpopulation and a tight little vacuum-packed family. Men and women live a long time these days, and they often keep having children just to give themselves an emotional outlet. (Many people in our culture seem able to express strong emotions—whether caresses or curses—only to their children or their dogs.) Now that the survival of the race depends upon most couples having not more than two children, it becomes particularly important that we broaden the bonds of affection to include more than just spouse, children and pets.

We need bigger, less well-defined "families." We need groups of friends and neighbors who are willing and able to share the strongest feelings, to share responsibility for the emotional needs of all the children in the group. Thus no one will be childless, no one will lack affection, and no one will be deprived of a rich and varied emotional and sensual life. The empirical evidence so far indicates that swapping bed partners does not work. But sexual exclusivity shouldn't mean (as it now does) emotional and sensual exclusivity. The new sexuality leads eventually to the creation of a family as wide as all mankind, that can weep together, laugh together and share the common ecstasy.

Chapter 4

hot and cool sex—closed
and open marriage

Anna K. and Robert T. Francoeur

SEXUAL MYTHS

Every culture is nourished by its own piebald collage of attitudes, images, expectations, and values, some quite congenial and others uncomfortably restless in the overall culture. In each culture a unique consciousness is woven, mostly by weavers unconscious of their raw materials, or even of the final social fabric into which they have plaited themselves. Threads rise out of the past, emerging sometimes gently, sometimes with twisted violence, but they inevitably combine their web to catch up their unwitting weavers in the final fabric.

What we propose to do in this essay is trace for you the beginning and the end of our cultural fabric. We want to examine the past, present, and future of one crucial thread in this fabric, the male/female relationship and the structure of marriage.

We Americans have no clear vision or image of where we are going. We hardly have any vision of the past either. In fact, our youth delight in the instantaneous present, scorning the past and shunning tomorrow. We need, then, an image of our past. We have to understand and appreciate the values, attitudes, and expectations of the past in which we are rooted. We need a social myth of the past. But we also need an image of the future, a social myth of values and expectations that will provide inspiration and direction as we and our culture evolve with cataclysmic pace.

At the 1973 Groves Conference on Marriage and the Family, one workshop was devoted to discussion of semantics, labels, and models which seem to be emerging in our culture. Labels and models are

"Hot and Cool Sex—Closed and Open Marriage" by Anna K. and Robert T. Francouer. This essay appears for the first time in this book.

almost an essential tool in every culture before we can understand and discuss novelties in human behavior. We have to relate the novel to what we know by experience. But first we must verbalize what we know by experience. We have to label and describe our past attitudes, values, and models in male/female relations before we can project and describe the attitudes, values, and expectations we seem to be working towards in sex and marriage.

In this context, Marshall McLuhan and George B. Leonard suggest a basic model in their earlier picture of "The Future of Sex." What we propose to do here is expand and develop the basic insight of McLuhan and Leonard into two detailed social myths: Hot Sex, which encompasses the sexual attitudes that have characterized our American and European cultures for the past century in particular, and Cool Sex, the futuristic image of where we seem to be headed.

HOT SEX

Some may bristle at the judgmental tone implied in labeling the sexual consciousness of most Americans and Europeans today as Hot Sex. But the label is appropriate as a cultural myth and stereotype provided we exercise caution. The portrait we propose here for Hot Sex is an abstraction, a composite. Do not expect to see all the portrait's details in the behavior of a single person you know well, be that individual a friend, enemy, spouse, or yourself. But each of us exhibits a variety of these Hot-Sex traits simply because we have all been raised in this culture and breathe its attitudes and values.

In the previous essay, McLuhan and Leonard sketched the roots of the Hot-Sex mentality [cf. also: Ruether, p. 42], so we need not cover again that important territory. What we need to go into are the details of the Hot-Sex attitudes, values, and expectations.

Hot Sex, like hot media, presents a very clearly defined picture. The anatomical precision of the blown-up Playmate of the Month with no genital or mammary detail left to the imagination is the ideal Hot-Sex female. In the male stereotype, the raw aggressiveness of Loren Hardeman I (whose very name has a Hot-Sex significance) offers an excellent model of the Hot-Sex male in Harold Robbins' novel *The Betsey*. The high definition of Hot-Sex masculinity and femininity is precisely the anonymity of genital interlocking, the belief that sex is nothing except penis and vagina.

A curious circus of obsessions and anxieties appears when sex is segregated from persons and from everyday life, when it is reduced to genitality. The Hot-Sex obsession with genital intercourse shows in our common, spontaneous equation of intimacy with genital intercourse. It turns up in our common, often expressed concern with the size of the penis or breast. Loren Hardeman's French playmate of the moment paid him the ultimate Hot-Sex compliment when "She stared at it in wonder. 'C'est formidable. Un vrai Canon!' "

Hot Sex is the American fascination with what appears to be an unlimited variety of "perfect" sexual techniques, positions, and combinations, all of which must be experienced if one is to be "with it." Hot Sex is the worried adolescent quest for mutual orgasm at all costs, the anxious, frantic search for multiple orgasm with the "perfect" partner, or, more honestly, the perfect organ. Hot-Sex relationships, like those in *The Last Tango in Paris,* are casual in their impersonalism: in the dark, one hole is the same as any other, one rod the same as any other—and often the same even when faced in the light of day. Hot Sex often merely moves the fig leaf to the face.

Hot Sex is curiously haunted by the virginal siren. Attraction and fear combine in the male's desire to be the first to deflower his property. Virginity, like the person you marry or are in love with, is basically a commodity. As a commodity, virginity is undamaged, intact property. As long as no penis has *violated* a girl's vaginal canal, or taken possession of it, she remains a virgin. She may very well have masturbated to mutual orgasm with a dozen males, but as long as no male has taken possession of her "innermost treasure," she remains *technically* a virgin. The wives in Bangladesh were quickly discarded by their husbands after their rape by invading soldiers: spoiled property is worthless. Male virginity, on the other hand, is frowned upon in a Hot-Sex culture—not unexpectedly since Hot Sex is patriarchal and holds to a double standard. The female's role is to provide man with his pleasure and comfort, as well as a domestic support system.

When human sexuality is segmented from life and clearly defined in terms of genitals, it naturally has to be scheduled, arranged, planned, both in time and place. The evolution of the bedroom (McLuhan/Leonard, p. 17), and the plotted affair pursued at night in some hidden motel are evidence of the explosive, volatile, and tenuous place Hot Sex holds in everyday life.

Hot Sex is *Last-Tango* screwing in the most depersonalized sex-object way. In classic style, Loren Hardeman "poised over her, like a giant animal blocking out the light until all she could see was him . . . as he slammed into her with the force of the giant body press she had seen working in his factory on a tour the day before."

In a Hot-Sex culture there is also a fig-leafed obsession with nudity and the naked female figure. Female nudity is accepted or tolerated for the sake of art, or the erotic enjoyment of the male, but male nudity is frowned upon. Even in the privacy of one's home and family circle, not infrequently even with one's spouse, the privacy of one's body is clothed from view.

Hot Sex is entropic, self-destructive, because it lives by *possessing* and conquering sex objects. It is entropic also because its life blood is the vital compulsion to perform: the destructive pressure on the male to screw every chance he gets and the equally destructive pressure on the female to satisfy the male ego with the benediction of a mutual orgasm, or better, of mutual and multiple orgasms.

Genital Hot Sex is an end unto itself: sex *for* fun, *for* ego satisfaction, *for* ego building. In Hot Sex one can escape the unbearable burden of time and aging simply by multiplying experiences. Like the passenger on the train in Marcel Proust's *Remembrance of Things Past,* the Hot-Sex male darts desperately from one window to the next, from one conquest to the next, in hopes of encompassing and proving his manhood in a good scorecard with ever mounting conquests.

The *real* sex in a Hot-Sex value system is the forbidden fruit, the thrill of cheating, the escape from boredom and routine of everyday relations into the romantic wonderland of an affair. Even in that modern version of the socially acceptable infidelity, the swinger and mate-swapper are not up to dealing with real involvement, real intimacy. The swinger allows genital infidelity, provided it does not involve persons. The swinger does not resolve his or her jealousy and instead retains a possessiveness that allows a temporary, safety-valve swing while still viewing any real intimacy as a threat and potential competition. Hot Sex views any human relationship in terms of competition and threat.

In a Hot-Sex culture, marital fidelity is reduced to what I did not do in Dubuque. Marital fidelity is synonymous with genital exclusivity. And since sexuality is implied in any intimacy, every sexually mature single person poses a threat. The unmarried, widowed, divorced, obviously are sex-starved because one cannot possibly be a fulfilled male or female without constant sexual genital experiences. Intimacy of any kind with the unmarried must be resolved (in the hypocrisy of American life) as soon as possible by marriage. Likewise, the extramarital relationship must be resolved either in divorce and remarriage, or in termination of the affair. With the forbidden-fruit romance of the affair weighting the value scale in favor of divorce and remarriage, a Hot-Sex culture can only view the single person as a threat to all married people.

In this same vein, couples exist—*not* sexually mature persons who happen also to be married. Couples go everywhere together. Married couples are safe because they are asexually symbiotic in their togetherness. They go everywhere with their spouses and would never think of leaving their spouse home and going out with another person of the opposite sex.

In a Hot-Sex culture based on propertied relations, it is the male, the husband, who is free and self-defined. Because a wife belongs to her husband, her identity is drawn from her husband. The father gives away his daughter at a wedding; no one gives away the groom. Many men continue to respond emotionally at even the suggestion of a threat to their property rights, as did one television personality in a discussion of open marriage: "I'll strangle the bastard who puts his paws on my property!"

Monogamy, life-long and sexually exclusive, is obviously the sole way of adult life (though the husband is allowed certain freedom and license not open to his wife). Every adult is urged, even compelled, into marriage as soon as possible. The slightest thought of an alternate to traditional monogamy is taboo, for monogamy (with the wife as a domestic support system) is the inviolable monolithic foundation of all our economics, politics, and social structure.

Hot Sex is dualistic and gnostic. It really despises or, at best, tolerates the body. The human body is enshrouded with countless taboos that restrict touching and body contact of all but the most "innocent" and "nonintimate" type. As a result, Hot Sex is sterile, antiseptic, and antisensual. It is cut off from the whole person, isolated from nature and the cosmos. For the earthy, cosmic myths of tribal, nomadic cultures with their cool-sex attitudes toward the body, the hot-sex mentality substitutes only the frail, treacherous lure of the great orgasm hunt, the Parsiphalian quest of the perfect partner with the perfect organ and technique, the *Love-Story* myth, and the belief that despite its segregation from life—and, in fact, because of this segregation—Hot Sex, genital sex, is IT.

In brief, Hot Sex is male-dominated, double-standarded, intercourse-obsessed, property-oriented, and clearly stereotyped in its sexist images and models.

COOL SEX

After centuries of gestating in our increasingly hot-sex culture, a new set of attitudes, values, and expectations is finally breaking through to the surface. This is happening not primarily, as the mass media and common image has it, among the college generation, but rather among those married couples in their thirties and forties, where a certain amount of financial independence has joined with the perspective only experience can bring to allow a critical look at their traditional Hot-Sex attitudes and expectations. The courtly love of medieval times and the Renaissance began the degenitalization of Hot Sex, setting the stage for an emasculation of American Hot Sex centuries later and putting the western world on the path to a new culture, the Leonard/McLuhan Cool Sex.

In this new framework, the relationship of men and women can once again be expressed validly as a peer relationship, between two evolving, maturing, sexual, and unique persons. In this Cool-Sex consciousness, men, and especially women, have to become conscious of themselves as individuals with a real existence outside their socially imposed, stereotyped roles. Men and women must realize that creation, our creation as human beings, is an ongoing process of becoming. In many respects, as Paul Klee suggested, "Becoming is superior to being." Masculinity and femininity cannot be defined clearly in a Cool-Sex culture because they are still in the process of being evolved by every sexual person individually. Maleness and femaleness are not subject to the high definition of a Hot-Sex culture. They are fluid realities, constantly changing and constantly being created, not as rigid archetypes but as scintillating process incarnations, each expression with its own unique value.

The consciousness of Cool Sex requires a degree of self-identity. Men or women must first of all be somewhat secure in their image of themselves as persons, without relying on the blessing of society's stereotypes. In Maslow's language, they must be self-actualizing and free of the need to borrow their identity and direction from society or another individual. The ability to stand alone, with some real degree of psychological and emotional maturity is essential to a Cool-Sex mentality.

Given the low definition of masculinity in Cool Sex, it is no longer possible for a man to judge his maleness and identity in terms of multiple conquests and (male) progeny. Nor can a woman find her identity as a person in the phrases "his wife" and "their mother," or in the number of times she has produced pattering feet [cf.: Binstock, p. 78, below].

Cool Sex means considering and accepting for others *and for oneself* the *real* possibility of alternatives to the traditional hot-sex stereotypes of breadwinner, housewife, parent, married *couple,* "good girl" (fair white maiden), and double standards. Since sexual persons in a cool-sex culture are not defined in terms of their roles, men and women are free to explore and express their own personalities with as little role playing as possible and with a minimum of imperatives other than the basic rule of not exploiting others in any way, as objects, sexual or otherwise.

Cool sexuality is expressed in integrated, holistic behavior which

accepts the human body wholeheartedly and fully. It is neither disturbed by nudity nor scandalized by "immodesty." Cool sexual consciousness celebrates the body in the tradition of Solomon's *Song of
Songs,* and the Woodstock–Watkins Glen generation. It is involved
and intimate, simultaneously inclusive and embracing rather than
exclusive, possessive, and jealous. It takes into consideration *all* the
needs and responsibilities of *all* the persons involved in or affected
by a relationship. It diffuses the genital spotlight over the whole body.
It tends to integrate a whole range of bodily intimacies, touching,
nudity, and sensuality, along with genital intercourse, into the total
framework of daily living.

Human relations guided by a Cool-Sex consciousness are synergistic, rather than entropic. Cool Sex means neither the end nor the
lack of emotions, intense feelings, concern, or warmth. What it does
mean is that relations are not taken in terms of possession or competition.

Marriage, in particular, is modified in a cool-sex culture. We are
convinced, despite the predictions of monogamy's impending doom,
of the value of long-term one-to-one commitments and relations. But
the self-destructive, unreal exclusiveness of the Victorian romantic
monogamy has got to change radically. We have already accepted in
our culture a major modification in one of the two basic values in
marriage. We have found it easier to modify our value of life-long
monogamy with no-fault divorce, divorce, and remarriage rather than
modify the exclusivity of traditional marriages. But we are beginning
to question whether this is the more humane and growth-oriented
adaptation. Its ease, when compared with exploring adaptations and
modifications in the traditional marital exclusivity, may destroy human relations and hinder personal growth far more than any modification in marital exclusivity. Our view is that long-term pair bonds
can evolve as primary relationships within the realistic context of
today's world with its increasing mobility, stretching life expectancies,
contraceptives, and the socioeconomic liberation of women.

In a Cool-Sex culture, the nuclear family and exclusive couple
will, more often than not, after about five years during which they
become secure in their own primary relationship, come to accept an
openness and flexibility unheard of in a Hot-Sex culture. This openness would accept a variety of intimate relations *on all levels,* for
both husband and wife, including the *possibility* of genitally expressed
relations, within the orbit of the primary relationship and comple-
menting it. This open, flexible type of marriage, with its multilateral
pluralism of intimacies, would be far more functional than the rigid
couple pattern of past generations, though it also involves certain

new psychological and emotional demands and risks which we have explored in detail in *Hot and Cool Sex: Cultures in Conflict* (1974) [cf. also: Lawrence, p. 66, below].

The Reverend William Genné, of the National Council of Churches' Family Life Bureau, and Drs. Rustum and Della Roy, authors of *Honest Sex,* several years ago coined the label *comarital* to describe a relationship which parallels, complements, and reinforces the primary relationship of a married couple. This comarital relationship may be a very personal and intimately emotional friendship, even one involving genital expression. More recently we have suggested the label of *satellite relationship* since the word *comarital* gives a bias toward the marital end and does not cover the situation in which a secondary relationship complements a primary nonmarital relationship. The need for, and function of, satellite relationships that complement long-term primary relations are based on the complexities of modern life, the varieties of educational backgrounds, and the inevitable, not necessarily parallel, growth and change in personal expectations. When one's education, expectations, and background are limited, it is fairly easy to find one person who can completely and totally meet your growth potential for life. With short life expectancies, most men and women were forced into serial monogamy with several mates by the early death of a spouse in childbirth, war, plague, or pestilence. Today, as our life span stretches and we become richer in background and expectations, it may well be that one person will be unable to meet all our changing needs over fifty or more years.

The choice for our generation, then, seems to fall between a traditional, sexually exclusive *series* of relationships—modular, monogamous marriages which explode after five or ten years when their Hot-Sex expectations are frustrated and unfulfilled—and, on the other side, some sort of open marriage based on the Cool-Sex attitudes which neither reduce marital fidelity to sexual exclusivity nor view one's partner as property.

The satellite relationship, however, only becomes possible when both partners in a primary relation are secure in their own self-identity and in their primary pair-bonding. Property can be lost, but a personal commitment is not necessarily destroyed by a secondary commitment. The satellite relation, then, is not the explosive affair, but a constructive, complementary relationship open to married and single persons, husbands and wives alike, in a context and social structure in which relations are synergistic, reinforcing, and strengthening rather than competitive and entropic.

This expansion of human relations to integrate new modes and expressions of intimacy and community within the couple marriage seems to recapture a consciousness that apparently found its way from the earliest aborigines into the early biblical tradition only to be lost as urbanization began its slow triumph in the Western Judaeo-Christian tradition. The early Hebrews had no words for sex or sexual intercourse until they borrowed these fragmenting terms and concepts from the more urban thinkers of Persia, Greece, and Rome. The original biblical tradition, and the Hebrew language even today, speaks of the engaging, pleasuring, person-integrating relationship between a man and woman not as "making love" nor as genital intercourse. Rather they used the simple, rich word *yahda* ("knowing"). This is no Victorian euphemism, but rather a clear indication of the holistic approach to human relations existing among the early nomadic Hebrews before patriarchal, sexist distinctions took over.

Few modern western writers have captured this cool-sex consciousness. Most of them cannot even deal with the present tensions of ordinary people caught in the transition from hot to cool. Witness, for instance, the inability of the gifted John Updike, both in *Couples* and *Rabbit Redux*, to deal with extramarital intimacies and relations in anything but a totally negative, threatening Hot-Sex framework.

Only in science fiction or the utopian essay/novels of Robert Rimmer do we catch some glimpse of what Cool-Sex attitudes and values might be. Rimmer's classic *The Harrad Experiment* and his latest novel, *Thursday, My Love,* are prime examples, as is Robert Heinlein's haunting *Stranger in a Strange Land.* Heinlein uses satire, humor, and fantasy to tell the story of Valentine Michael Smith, the son of the first humans to land on Mars. After being raised and educated by Martians when his parents died, Mike returns to this earth with a later expedition only to be shocked by the Hot-Sex mentality of earthlings. The Martian pattern of male-female relations he knew was communal and multisensual, with no sharp cultural distinction between male and female roles. What earthlings call sexual intercourse and reduce to genital coupling, Mike views as "grokking" or "growing closer," a kind of demierotic relating and interpersonal knowing in the original biblical sense.

Similar examples turned up in the cinema in the early 1970s. *The Graduate, The Summer of '42,* and *Carnal Knowledge* contain beautiful expressions of the Hot- and Cool-Sex myths in their main characters.

In books about human sexual behavior, *The Joy of Sex,* which Alexander Comfort edited for Crown Publishers (1973), is outstanding. Its line drawings and soft, detailed illustrations communicate a cool-sex mentality better than any other book of this type we know.

In facing the problems of language and new words to describe our emerging values and attitudes, it is well to recall that in most tribal and aboriginal cultures, there is no word for illegitimacy because all children are considered as young persons in their own right and not the property of any set of parents. Often too, because of the parity of men and women in tribal cultures, there is no word for adultery. Social taboos do limit sexual behavior for the good of the community, but not because the wife or daughter is the property of some male.

Cool Sex, then, is egalitarian, single-standarded, sensually-diffused, and oriented towards intimacy and open, synergistic relations with persons.

HOT AND COOL SEX, CLOSED AND OPEN MARRIAGE

We have discovered some fascinating parallels between our social models of Hot and Cool Sex and the descriptions of Closed and Open Marriage proposed by anthropologists Nena and George O'Neill in *Open Marriage*.

With the help of friends at Sandstone, a unique Cool-Sex experiment in California, we worked out an itemized list of characteristics for Hot and Cool Sex. In a chapter on "Synergy," the O'Neills also itemize the details of Closed and Open Marriages. Rearranging the O'Neills' tables and ours on the basis of 1) definitions, 2) value systems, 3) behavioral structures, and 4) concerns produces a very informative picture:

Definitions:

Hot Sex: high definition; clear sex-role stereotyping; sex equated with genital coupling; segregation of sex in time and place; numerous strong imperatives from society; highly structured with many "games."
Closed Marriage: static framework; rigid role prescriptions; highly calculating; change is threatening.
Cool Sex: low definition; sexuality coextensive with personality; diffused sensuality; spontaneous; light structure and few social games; few social imperatives; little, if any role stereotyping; self-actualization encouraged.
Open Marriage: dynamic framework; flexible in its roles; adaptable to change; spontaneous.

Value Systems:

Hot Sex: patriarchal, with aggressive male dominating passive female; double moral standard.

Closed Marriage: unequal status of husband and wife; selfhood subjugated to couplehood; bondage.

Cool Sex: equalitarian; partnership; friendship; single moral standard.

Open Marriage: equality of stature; personal identity; freedom.

Behavioral Structures:

Hot Sex: property-oriented; possessively closed; casual and impersonal; physical sex segregated from life, emotions, and responsibility; grossly selective of playmates; screwing sex objects for conquest; genital hedonism.

Closed Marriage: couples locked together; smothering, with limited growth potential; possession shuts out others; closed, self-limiting energy system.

Cool Sex: person-oriented; open; inclusive; involved and intimate; sex integrated in everyday life; finely selective in all relations; sex viewed as communications and "knowing" sexual persons.

Open Marriage: openness between spouses; freedom that incorporates others; growth-oriented, open companionships; privacy for self-growth; individual autonomy in an open, expanding energy system.

Concerns:

Hot Sex: orgasm-obsessed; performance pressures; fidelity means sexual exclusivity; extramarital relations are an escape; nudity taboo; emotions and senses feared; sexuality basically feared; entropic because property can be used up; alcohol and drug-altered states common; personal space a prime concern.

Closed Marriage: limited love; deception and game-playing; conditional, static trust; exclusion of others; inhibitive; degenerative and subtractive relations in a closed, self-limiting energy system.

Cool Sex: engaging, pleasuring communications; sexual relations accepted but truly optional; fidelity means commitment and responsibility; comarital relations, with or without genital expression, growth reinforcing; senses and emotions embraced; nudity, even in groups, optional; synergistic relationships; grokking; drug-altered states not common.

Open Marriage: honesty; truth; open love; open trust; openness to others; creativeness; expansive and additive relations in an open, expanding energy system.

Within the emerging pluralism of male-female relations in our global city, many patterns of marriage will be increasingly tolerated because some people find them functional. However, we are convinced that the majority of people will find themselves confronted with a choice between two patterns. One of these is the traditional romantic, patriarchal, sexually exclusive marriage which will adapt to the new environmental system of today and tomorrow by modification in practice, if not immediately in theory. Multiple divorce and remarriage, serial polygamy, will be the result, with all the other attitudes, values, and expectations of the Hot-Sex myth retained. The alternative will be some sort of flexible, dynamic Open Marriage with a new dynamic definition of fidelity as "loving concern" and commitment. In this second pattern, "forsaking all others" will be the element of traditional marriage that is modified.

The question is which modification will be the most humane, most functional, most growth-promoting, and for which people. Not all can handle the Cool-Sex values and attitudes, nor will all continue to opt for the Hot-Sex values and attitudes. The trend, however, is definitely towards pluralism in our marital patterns, with the growing popularity of new values of fidelity and commitment, new risks and new challenges.

Chapter 5

the personalization of sexuality

Rosemary Reuther

Why is it that cultures, for as long as one can remember in history, have depersonalized and brutalized human sexuality? Despite some years of reflection and a year of intensive research on the history of sexual ideology in Western religion and society, this question remains an enigma to me.

As a Catholic child I was given an indoctrination intended to instill an instinctive sense of fear and horror of my own stirring sexual feelings. But like other things I heard in those days from priests and nuns, this was one of those things that I never really believed. (I remember as a teenager being told by a nice young Irish priest in the confessional that I should pray for "purity." I remember thinking to myself, "that's your problem, not mine. You pray for purity. I'll pray for other things.")

On the other hand, a casual, depersonalizing use of sex also discomfited me. My mother's late Victorian romanticism taught me, in a vague way, that this was all supposed to be "for" something much more "beautiful."

The root of this great fear of sexuality in culture, which has wasted so much of our moral energies, failed to make sense to me. What are people really afraid of? Are men really *that* afraid of women? Are men afraid that if women are really free to be sexual, they will be shown to be much less than the "he-men" the male ideology demands? Are we all—men and women—somehow afraid of our own bodies? Why is sexual feeling posed as a threat that symbolizes the destruction of the mental and moral self "from below"? This is the way both Christian asceticism and Freudianism have presented the issue to us. Sexual feeling is seen as the bestial self that must be repressed and controlled so that intellect, spirit and the "higher virtues" can dominate. Sexual repression is seen as the necessary price that must be paid for the emergence of the higher self.

Recently I have come to suspect that this way of presenting the problem is a defense stratagem that covers up what people really fear. Perhaps what people are most afraid of is not so much the indulgence of feeling as the communication of the inner self. Sex, depersonalized, allows us to avoid the challenge of using our whole self, our total energies and feelings, to present and communicate ourselves to another. Sex is the victim of the fear of love.

A philosopher, recently in love, wrote me in response to an early draft of this article that men fear love because it is similar to a "death experience." Sexual experience, for him, is connected somehow with loss of the self. To open oneself to deep vulnerability and communication is profoundly terrifying. This becomes more terrifying when it is unified with sexual experience as a total body-possibility where communication becomes ecstasy.

I don't know whether many men really experience sex in this way. It seems to have much more to do with the way men experience sex than with the way women experience it. But if this is true, it may suggest the subconscious dynamics that cause men to hold back from really communicating themselves in sexual experience. The old tactic of splitting the self from the body and manipulating the body as an instrument of experience, without really disclosing and communicating the self in this act, is typical of a male sexuality that demands, as its complement, the depersonalization of the woman. The dream of ecstatic love inspires poets. But, in actuality, we shrink from such an experience because it demands moral development and creativity; a self-searching and self-giving that finds the deepest I-Thou at the point where the ego dissolves its defenses.

DEBASING SEXUALITY: REPRESSING THE BODY

This vision of total, ecstatic self-giving and communicating has also dominated religious mysticism. But religion pulled the inner experience away from its sexual foundation to sublimate it into a vision of contemplative ecstasy that expressed the quest for God. To explore that possibility experientially as a real relationship with another person concretizes that possibility. Sexuality signifies the potential for ecstasy in interpersonal relations. But we constantly betray this possibility by sublimating our ecstatic power and depersonalizing our body and that of the other. Sexuality is debased to ward off the challenge of love.

Historically, there have been two ways of debasing sexuality: the ascetic and the libertine. The ascetic represses physical experience and withdraws in revulsion from both his own body and those of others, especially women. He makes ecstasy an interior experience between "God" and the "bridal soul." All the erotic language of the Song of Songs was ransacked in traditional Christian mysticism to provide the language of this ecstatic communication between the soul and its divine "lover."

The various modern efforts to revolt against classical asceticism reproduced remnants of the same repressive culture. The romantic also avoided bodily contact and held out a faith in a better and higher interpersonality between men and women to be achieved "spiritually." Women had to be kept sexually innocent so they could function as the pure love object of one's dreams. The very idea that your father had sexual intercourse with your mother to produce you became an unmentionable social scandal in Victorian times.

In ascetic culture sex hardly disappears as a fact of life. Instead, it must be placed in a depersonalized sphere where it can make no spiritual demands. The body is objectified as an alien, dangerous force that one must repress. What this means is that a lower sphere is marked out where one can "capitulate" to this force, but in a way that can never be integrated into the moral, responsible self. Widespread prostitution was the "other world" the Victorians created to compensate for the sublimated idealism of their relations with "respectable women."

DEBASING SEXUALITY: SUBORDINATING WOMEN

A power relation of supra- and subordination between men and women is essential to this schism. Only by making one person in the relationship inferior, dependent and "purely carnal" can one assure a sexuality without the demands of interpersonality. By making woman body, one does not have to relate to her as a person. In this respect asceticism is the extreme nadir of patriarchalism.

This has the effect not of preventing the ascetic from giving in to sex but rather of assuring that this experience will always be treated as "sin." As soon as one is able to gain control over oneself, one must repress this experience, repent and return to sublimated "purity." The female sexual partner is identified essentially with sin and treated as a wanton lower being to be repudiated as soon as one can repudiate "sin." The love-ecstasy potential of sexuality is seen as something fundamentally other than the body. It is fantasized as a purely interior relationship that is possible only when one withdraws from the evil realm of the body, the woman and the world, and devotes oneself solely to "God."

However, with the end of the Victorian era, there came a continuing revolt against these ways of sublimating sexuality. The split between idealized love in the family and debased sex in the "other world" of the Victorian brothel began to disappear. Women began to reclaim their rights to sexual experience [cf. McLuhan and Leonard, p. 17, above].

At first this newly sexualized, middle-class female was seen as a profound threat to "home and family." But gradually it became apparent that the sexualizing of women could be as effective in tying women to their traditional domestic and sexual roles in male-dominated society as had been the earlier sexual repression of women. Sexual liberation, defined in male terms as the availability of women for sexual exploitation, is the primary way that Freudian culture has diverted the demands of the first woman's movement for full personhood. Sexualized woman is exploited to sell every product of commercial bourgeois culture in a way that constantly enforces her domestication and subordination to male power.

Even in the student culture and the New Left, presumably in revolt against the bourgeois family, the same view of women prevailed. Radical women in the sixties received a painful but galvanizing shock when they realized that, in the words of Stokely Carmichael, "the only place for women in the Movement is prone." Women in the Movement realized that they had been betrayed into a "sexual liberation" defined primarily in terms of their being available for male "relief of concupiscence" (to use the traditional Christian language!) but little concerned with their personal liberation. Sexual libertinism showed its true colors as simply an alternative strategy for avoiding the challenge of love.

Sex was to be freely accepted as something that could be done "whenever you feel like it." But the split between the self and the body did not disappear. One used one's own body and exploited that of the other person for sexual experience. But self-disclosure, personal relations and communication were withheld as much as ever. In the "liberated relationship" women found themselves angrily charged with having "hang-ups" if they wanted this experience to signify personal affection, commitment or deep communion. Women found themselves subjected to an interpretation of sexual liberation that meant physical experience without "getting involved." It became apparent that this was possible only by maintaining the traditional power relations of men over women and by relegating women to the status of domestic servant and body-object. The new Woman's Movement grew out of this shock.

Today the Woman's Movement is still confused over the relationship between sexual liberation and women's liberation. Women have little desire to retreat to the celibacy of the women of the first woman's movement. They intend to retain the rights to sexual experience that were gained by the revolt against Victorianism in the 20th century. But now this sexual liberation must be centered in personal liberation. The autonomy, dignity and wholeness of a woman as a person must now become the center from which a woman operates sexually. The split between self and body that demands either repression or exploitation of women and the body must be overcome. Only when sexual liberation is united with women's liberation can sexual experience become reunified as a total communication between two persons.

DEBASING SEXUALITY: REPRESSING CONSCIOUSNESS

The current mores of American culture manifest the deep dislocations that occur when a gospel of sexual liberation is proclaimed that still retains the mind-body split and demands the traditional powerlessness and domestication of women. We now take for granted that the sexual experience of married couples should be full of "good orgasms." But American married couples grow increasingly disappointed with their sexual lives. This disappointment is carefully pointed away from its real source by treating it always as a mechanical and functional problem. Sex clinics have grown up around the country to help people become more skillful in the "mechanics" of sex, so they can get more mileage out of each other as stimulators of orgasmic experience.

But the quest for orgasmic experience is steered away from ever touching on the real core of the self. One still makes love with genitals, not selves. Just as asceticism tried to hang on to a self-enclosed ego by repressing the body as dirty, so does "sexual liberation" seem equally determined to eclipse mind, spirit and personhood so that one can really "feel." A kind of repression of consciousness and debasing of personality seems to be the contemporary way of avoiding the challenge of love, just as body-repression was in the past [cf. Callahan, p. 107, below].

Asceticism also mechanized sex by insisting that, whereas the "spiritual people" should withdraw from sex, the "carnal" married ones should "use" it solely as the means for procreation. Sex was reduced to a function or a means of producing a product, a baby! The very possibility of experiencing sexuality as a vehicle of personal communication was obliterated through the ascetic antithesis. Sex as a good in itself, rather than a mechanized means of procreation, was defined morally out of bounds. The Church Fathers regarded non-procreative sex as mere capitulation to bestiality.

The erotic experience, even if dutifully procreative, was in fact regarded as sin anyway by the Church Fathers. But it was a "forgiven sin" because of its "good end" in procreation. This end, however, was still considered tainted by "original sin," which adhered intrinsically to orgasmic experience. Through the "taint" of that experience—which the married couple could not restrain but must be taught to despise—original sin was transmitted to the child. The child was born "dirty" as a result of its "dirty" means of creation! In this way one kept from ever recognizing that the real demoralization of sex takes place in its reduction to procreative functionality. The reduction of women to submissive, carnal bodiliness was also essential to this depersonalizing of sex in the ascetic definition of marital "morality."

Marriage has traditionally assured the modicum of support and subsistence for the persons so used for their sexual functions. But until the dawn of modern society cultures seldom tried to unify love with marriage. In medieval Christian civilization love was seen as possible only outside marriage. In traditional societies the wife was quickly worn out with childbearing. Even sexual release, for men, took place mostly outside of marriage. It was the revolution of modern bourgeois morality that tried to unify marriage and love. At first this took a highly sublimated form, for Christian asceticism taught Western man that there was an unbridgeable split between love and sex. The eroticized marriage of post-Freudian culture only adds a further stress to a system that still demands the dependency and domestication of women.

THE NUCLEAR FAMILY

Modern moralists are wont to bemoan the "decline of the family," as though such a notion of the family has existed from the dawn of history and has fallen into trouble only recently. But, in fact, such a notion of marriage is a product of an evolution that began in the late Medieval-Reformation period with a recovery of biblical familialism, and only in this century did it reach its present form. Modern marriage is under stress because never before in history has such a high demand been put on it as the unique realm of interpersonal fulfillment. In addition to continuing all of its traditional patriarchal demands of fidelity and domestic service, the wife must now be the total companion and the sexual playmate of her spouse. And she must do this in a framework that often offers few horizons beyond the nursery and the kitchen, with their adjunct suburban institutions.

It is now assumed that married couples should stay together only as long as they are really friends. But such a marriage neither guarantees nor necessarily nurtures friendship. Sexual partnership and a domestic institution held together for security and for the sake of the children, with a brutalized sex that expresses little or no human communication, is, to a greater or lesser degree, the state of many marriages. This is the legitimized immorality of marital sexuality that patriarchal religion and psychology are totally incapable of treating.

The only system that can guarantee sexual morality is one that is not built on the debasement of women. Such a system would assume the right of personal development for each partner. It would assume that their covenant with each other is a commitment to friendship and communication. It assumes that one partner is not forced into a state of dependency and underdevelopment for the sake of a male-dominated autonomy and work culture.

Modern marriage has virtually lost all of its former social and economic functions; it exists now for the nurture of children and as the arena of intense interpersonality. But just because all other forms of work have been eliminated from the function of marriage, it has become emotionally overloaded by concentrating on these two functions. To make deep friendship the sole basis for founding the institution where children are nurtured, in the highly intensive way characteristic of child-oriented culture, becomes increasingly contradictory.

THE SEARCH FOR ALTERNATIVES

Thus the final development of the nuclear family results today in a frantic search for alternatives. One seeks some larger communal structure that can guarantee personal community and a community for child-raising within which one can seek deep personal friendship and can explore the unification of personal and sexual communication. But the ability to achieve such communication should not be the sole basis for maintaining the institution that provides shelter, security and the nurturing of children.

Also, a deep personal covenant between two persons should not totally exclude the possibility of another sexual-love relationship at the same time. One should be able to be open to the possibility of more than one sexual friendship without this exploding the foundation of the family. But this is impossible within the structure of a family psychology whose sole basis is sexual friendship conceived of as a totalitarian form of exclusive private possession [cf.: Francoeur, p. 30; Comfort, p. 52; Lawrence, p. 66].

The youth culture is much concerned with discovering nonpossessive relationships. But the free love of that culture has only begun to suggest alternatives to the nuclear family as the arena of personal security, friendship and child-raising. As long as this culture does not take seriously the question of a community of adults and children, it contributes little to a significant critique of the present form of the family. On the other hand, its notions of nonpossessive love readily deteriorate to the level of the pre-existing uncommitted, depersonalized sexism. "Authentic relationship," as the sole criterion of sexual morality, is belied by a culture that, itself, uses the word "fuck" as a synonym for dehumanized exploitation. The threat of sex as a vehicle of love is warded off with new stratagems of depersonalization, with some disappointment, but also with some relief. Self and soma again fall apart into self-enclosed ego and depersonalized body.

Perhaps the unification of sexuality with love is finally unsolvable in a mass culture or by institutionalized relationships. Profound interpersonal development cannot be guaranteed by social structures or generalized acculturation. Sexuality as love remains a deeply creative development of communication between two persons. If we can open ourselves to the beloved on the deepest level and make our body-selves the sacrament of personal communication, the result will be the transfiguration of our total creative powers that must restore to our sexuality those deepest powers of personality hitherto alienated as the "spiritual realm." Even in our best relationships, we fall away from this redeemed moment most of the time—either through the abstraction of consciousness from the body-presence or through the alienation of the somatic self as an alien object, to be feared or used, but not really integrated into our persons. Both of these forms of inner schism express our inability to communicate with and care about the other persons whom we touch most intimately with our minds and bodies.

marriage

" 'Morals,' in their usual and sexual meaning, reflect in rules the culture's image of what the family should be." But what will those rules and morals be, Alex Comfort asks, when our society achieves a zero-growth population? Will we accept three forms of sexual relations: sex for parenthood, sex for total intimacy in a pair-bond relation, and sex for play and recreation? With fewer and fewer children and blood lines ever narrower, will we use sexual relationships to express new forms of kinship and intimacy? Comfort offers some provocative projections along these lines. He believes that our society will continue its tendency to "institutionalize" adultery or extra- and co-marital relations. He sees jealousy, a distinct offspring of the patriarchal, property-oriented marriage of Victorian times, becoming "emotionally unintelligible." All of which would make for an interesting world in terms of human growth and the individual. The social repercussions of this new image of sexuality touch every facet of our civilization's institutions, but first and foremost, they will lead us to a new image of the basic intimacy of pair-bonding we traditionally call monogamy and marriage.

Canadian sociologist Leo Davids deals with our initial steps today toward two principles which he believes will characterize our model of marriage in 1990: the legal freedom to personally and explicitly contract the type of marriage we choose, and formal public or communal control over parenthood. He begins by examining the forces of secularization, mobility, and the economic liberation of women as they undercut the traditional legal status of patriarchal monogamy. He then plunges into some speculations about new forms of courtship, the legalization of different forms of marital contracts, and, most controversially, the legal sanctions and controls we can expect society to place on parenting.

The completely negative image of extramarital relations has been a dominant theme in American fiction and everyday life. The extramarital relationship is "an affair," "cheating," "adultery," "infidelity," a sure sign one does not really love his or her spouse, a clear indication something serious is wrong with the marriage. Cheating is prelude to divorce and a new exclusive bond with the predatory "other woman or man." Affairs and monogamy are lethal opponents.

Recent decades have seen a new image begin to surface. In 1948 and 1953 Alfred Kinsey included some questions on extramarital experiences in his classic studies. Though these surveys were non-random and biased, their results gave the first concrete evidence that some Americans find extramarital relations a positive experience that complements and strengthens their marriages. In *The Significant Americans* (1965), Cuber and Harroff came to very pointed conclusions about the positive character of some extramarital relations among upper-middle class Americans. A year later sociologist Robert Whitehurst presented a paper at the annual convention of the National Council on Family Relations which he entitled: "Adultery as an Extension of Normal Behavior." In 1968 Rustum and Della Roy added an important religious dimension to the analysis of comarital relationships in their book *Honest Sex*.

This important religious perspective has not been explored in depth beyond the Roys' initial venture. How can adultery be a "faithful activity"? How do people in an extramarital relationship cope with their loss of innocence, their patent violation of the Judaeo-Christian ethic which underlies our American culture whether we are churchgoers or not? How can we relate today's emphasis on personal growth and autonomy for spouses with our pervasive religious image of sexual fidelity patterned on the fidelity of the religious person to one God: the equation of monogamy with monotheism? Fortunately, a member of the clergy has finally tackled these questions. Drawing on years of experience as an Episcopal priest, hospital chaplain, and marriage counselor, Raymond Lawrence takes a very practical look at the positive side of extramarital, comarital or satellite relationships. His rare candor and commonsense make his essay a milestone in the literature on American marriage in the '70s.

Chapter 6

sexuality in a zero growth society

Alexander Comfort

We are on the verge, in developed countries, of a society in which zero population growth will be an overriding social objective. Few people will have more than two children, and many will have none. By the mid 2000's people will probably live and remain vigorous longer through the control of natural aging. It will be a new game with different rules. The concept of the family which will alter—and is already altering—is that which folklore still maintains as our ideal expectation—the exclusive, totally self-sufficient couple-relationship, involving the ideal surrender of identity and of personal selfhood, which excluded kin and only grudgingly included children. The expectation, implied in so many novels and films, was in fact only rarely fulfilled. Unlike the older pattern, where there were other and supporting satisfactions beside each other's company, it was often a neurotic expectation. Young people today see this, and without diminishing their capacity for love, shy away from the idea of total self-surrender: "I am I and you are you, and neither of us is in this world to live up to the other's expectations . . . I love you, but in forty years we may be different people." This view, if not romantic, is at least realistic in terms of human experience.

Yet another change is that contraception has for the first time wholly separated the three human uses of sex—sex as parenthood, sex as total intimacy between two people ("relational" sex), and sex as physical play ("recreational" sex). "Morals," in their usual and sexual meaning, reflect in rules the culture's image of what the family should be. Religion, which in our culture traditionally rejects pleasure as a

"Sexuality in a Zero Growth Society" by Alexander Comfort. Reprinted with permission from the December, 1972, issue of the *Center Report,* a publication of the Center for the Study of Democratic Institutions, Santa Barbara, California.

motive, has tried hard to fence in the use of recreational sex. Until lately it did this by asserting that reproduction was the only legitimate use of sexuality. With the growth of the image of the ideal couple, it changed its ground, rather behind the event, so that today, together with many of its later successors in psychiatry and counseling, it asserts that worthy sex can only be relational. There has been no time in human history when either of these valuations was wholly true, though they have served in their time to reinforce the uses which that time made of the family. Even in the most strongly kin-based cultures, gaps were left for sexual activity which was not an expression either of a wish for children or of an all-embracing personal relationship. Such gaps concerned chiefly the male, who was often the legislator, and who claimed the right to experience sexual relations in a non-relational way, while excluding women from doing so, either by moral codes, or by the indoctrination of girls with the idea that relational sex is the sole kind of which women, as opposed to men, are capable.

The Pill has altered that. Secure from unwanted pregnancy, an increasing number of women have discovered that their capacity to experience sex at all three levels, either together or on different occasions and in different contexts, is as great as a man's, if not greater. The adult of today has all three options—sex as parenthood, sex as total relationship, and sex as physical pleasure accompanied by no more than affection. Older people looking at the young today realize increasingly how much the confusion between these modes, which they could not foresee, or even choose voluntarily between, has often complicated their lives; when play between boy and girl resulted in pregnancy and a forced marriage between mere acquaintances, when one partner misread the other's degree of involvement, or falsified his own selfishly to overcome reluctance.

Greater choice can bring greater problems and greater opportunities. It will bring problems in any event, and these can only be reduced by recognizing how great is the range of situations in which sex relations now take place, and learning to handle them to meet our own and our partner's needs. If we can do this, then the new freedom, though it now seems to be generating confusion, could reshape our living to meet the needs which were once met by the traditional human family pattern. We have dispensed with kin—to support us in life and look after us in old age. Consequently we are lonely, and we go to "sensitivity groups" to relearn how to treat people as people. The fantasy-concept of total one-to-one sufficiency has let us down. Since sex is now divorced from parenthood, there are many more relationships into which it can enter if we choose.

All that can be certainly predicted for the future is that the variety of patterns will increase as individuals find the norm that suits them. For some, parenthood will still be the central satisfaction, carrying with it the obligation of giving the children the stability they require. For others sexuality will express total involvement with one person. For others, one or more primary relationships will be central, but will not exclude others, in which the recreational role of sex acts as a source of bonding to supply the range of relationships formerly met by kin—an old human pattern in which sexual contacts were permitted between a woman and all her husband's clan brothers, or a man and all his wife's titular sisters.

In the zero population growth world we are all "clan brothers" and will have to find ways of expressing the hippy ideal of universal kinship. For many of the young today, a wider range of permitted sexual relationships seems to express this ideal, and even the rather compulsive wife-swapping of middle-aged couples in urban America seems to be reaching toward the same solution. What is clear is that we cannot reimpose the old rigidities. In going forward to newer and more varied patterns, our sense of responsibility and our awareness of others is going to be severely tested if we are not to become still more confused and unhappy. If we pass the test, we may evolve into a universal human family in which all three types of sex have their place, in which we are all genuinely kin, and in which all but the most unrealistic inner needs can be met in one form or another.

Conventional morals are probably correct in asserting that all satisfactory sex is in some degree inherently relational—if it is satisfactory, and mutually so, a relation subsists. Only the wholly insensitive mate mechanically, even under the conditions of permitted nondiscrimination which characterize a ritual orgy. A society like ours, which has traditionally feared and rejected close personal contact, has also generated a mythology of all-or-none involvement which profoundly influences us to our hurt. Unable to exclude the recreational and the partly relational modes of sex, it has set about rejecting or falsifying them. Once rid of this ideology, it might find that the relation present in purely recreational or social sex is a uniquely effective tool in breaking down personal separateness—of which the proprietary notion of love is an offshoot—so that, for us as for many primitives, social sex comes to express and cement the equivalent of kinship through a general intimacy and non-defensiveness, reinforced by the very strong reward of realizing suppressed needs for variety and for acceptance.

Our society has moved illogically in this direction by virtually institutionalizing adultery: a growing number of spouses permit each other complete sexual liberty on the conditions that there shall be no "involvement" and that the extracurricular relations are not brought to their attention. It is beginning to institutionalize ritual spouse exchange. This is more honest, and a better bet anthropologically;

non-involvement is, as it were, written in, the exchange is non-secret, and the partners, instead of excluding each other, share in the arrangement. How far conventional middle-class "swingers" profit emotionally in openness from their swinging is arguable—most studies suggest that they keep it in a watertight compartment and ritualize it as a sort of charismatic hobby or secret society, which embodies all current prejudices and does little to create any universal openness. At least, however, it marks the end, or the beginning of the end, of proprietary sexual attitudes. In part it has spread to the middle-aged from the young; older couples want to imitate their freedom without abandoning present attitudes. Unless the result disturbs children and leads to a backlash generation, the genuine insight present in "swinging" by the bored and the unrealized could expand into something far more like institutionalized sociosexual openness.

This process, so far as it has gone, would have been impossible without a gradual change in attitudes toward, and anxiety about, bisexuality. Mate-sharing, both psychoanalytically, and in primate ethology, reveals a surrogate sexual relation between males—expressed covertly so far in the gang night out and the attraction of the prostitute or "shared" woman, acceptable substitutes for overt male-male contacts because they are covert. The potential for more open bisexual contacts is greatly increased by two-couple activity. Men tend still to be disturbed by this, but women, who are in general less anxious about their bisexual potential, often embrace the opportunity with male encouragement. In fact, judging from primates, the state of sharing with another male, which reinforces individual dominance, could well help rather than hinder the heterosexuality of anxious people—dominance anxiety plays a large part in the suppression of heterosexual drives in most persons who regard themselves as constitutionally homosexual. Beside reinstating the kinship of men and women, a wider and opener use of sexuality is quite likely to reinstate, and reinforce, the kinship between men and men, which we now studiously avoid erotizing or expressing. In a fully erotized society, bisexuality, expressed or not, could cease to be a problem simply because social attitudes have changed.

Another important causalty of this process is likely to be sexual jealousy. Much argument has been devoted to discussing how far jealousy is a normal emotion, the counterpart of love, and how far it is a product of indoctrination. It would probably be true to say that in the traditional family jealousy was based on reproduction (knowing that my children are mine) and ideas of property, while in the romantic couple situation it is a product of the fear of rejection implicit in a surrender so alarmingly total. Modern attempts to transcend jealousy through wife-exchange or greater tolerance of affairs are often uncertain and anxious, but they have positive features—acceptance of a more realistic view of the needs of couples and individuals for variety, and recognition that the meeting of needs rather than their frustration is a gift which expresses love rather than devalues it, and strengthens the primary bond. (One need not be like the mischievous lovers of *"Les Liaisons Dangereuses"* to recognize this.) Such a recognition is important as marking the end of the mutual proprietorship, physical or emotional, which has so often characterized human sexual relationships in the past, and which modern woman, as well as modern man, rightly rejects as neurotic and immature. To our grandchildren, nineteenth century opera may be emotionally unintelligible.

Some will feel that the use of wider sex as a substitute for kinship devalues love and will leave us emotionally shallow. Others will see it as the defusing of a dangerous fantasy concerning the total nature of human love, which no society has enacted in fact or found satisfactory in the enactment, but which the folklore of the post-kinship family has wished on us to our hurt. The relationships of the zero growth society will have to be relationships between whole, adult people, dependent on their own resources, not using kin, family and children as a bolthole or one another as climbing-posts, but if this kind of adulthood can be attained at all widely (it will never be practicable for all) it could lead to relations far more supportive in a truly human sense than any we have so far known. Certainly none of the past fictions embodied in our stereotypes of male and female sex roles, of totally exclusive love, or even of central parenthood can readily persist unaltered.

We are not here talking about change which we can further or prevent, simply about changes which are now taking place. If we approach them on the basis of anxiety, past expectation and folklore they will only generate more of the anomie which we have now. The alternative is to see whether we can approach them with insight and compassion for one another.

Extension of survival into old age has already led to the concept of "two lifespans," with a second, adolescence-like identity crisis around the age of 40, when realized and unrealized goals are reassessed: the crisis may end in a resumption of established relationships, illness or depression, or a total recasting of relationships. The crisis is more prominent in men—their societal opportunity for a "new start," occupationally and sexually, is the greater—and it often leads to the starting of a second family with a younger partner. Women's opportunities are more cruelly circumscribed at this age—they tend to find themselves deserted, having "run out of" family and an established role. Any further extension of vigorous life through interference with aging might put them on a more equal footing with men; it will certainly increase the tendency for life-styles, and families, to be serial, so that each individual has the option of continuing in one pattern, or of entering a wholly different one, at the age when in the traditional family one was preparing for dependent senescence. The decline of the kinship family has borne excessively hard on the old— dependency is rejected, and they become increasingly isolated in a forced "independence" which is worsened by the shortage of kin. Perhaps more than anyone they would benefit from a "spreading" of the couple-preoccupied family into something more like a tribe of friends.

I would expect accordingly to see a society in which pair relationships are still central, but initially less permanent, in which childbearing is seen as a special responsibility involving a special life style, and in which settled couples engage openly in a wide range of sexual relations with friends, with other couples, and with third parties as an expression of social intimacy, without prejudice to the primacy of their own relationship, and with no more, and probably less, permanent interchange than we see in the society of serial polygamy with adultery that now exists. Such a pattern is coming into existence in America, and is beginning to become explicit. Whether it will devalue relationships or only deprive them of neurotic compulsion will depend on the persons involved, the amount of support they receive from the social ethic, and the accuracy of the expectations with which they enter maturity. If these expectations become realistic, it will be the first time that a modern generation has been reared with confidence but without illusions.

The political implications of universalized kinship are interesting. Marcuse, in discussing the "erotization of relationships" as a political force was once challenged to "go erotize the state of Kansas." My suggestion is that this may in fact be happening. The family is in fact the microcosm of politics with a one to two generation timelag. Institutional politics today reflect combative paternalism, which had its family counterpart in the 1850's, and liberal politics the social expression of the ideal of individualist romantic love. It is possible to overstate the inherently revolutionary potential of "universal kinship," but if, as I suggest, it is explicitly erotized, it will find a counterpart socially in anarchic community action. How far it produces such action, and how far the nonpossessive individual and the anti-authoritarian society are products of the same change in social requirement it is hard to say. The acceptance of sensuality, and the widening of its focus to include not one but many others, would seem in itself to be an emotional technology capable of fitting well into the less compulsive and more gentle world view of the twenty-first as against the nineteenth and twentieth centuries. Marcuse is probably right in seeing justice, non-possession, non-exploitation, ecology and the wider erotization of relationships as possible correlates. We may have a rough few years ahead before this pattern emerges, but when and if it does, one could wish to live in those times.

Chapter 7

new family norms

Leo Davids

It is marriage that has been changing profoundly in recent decades, not just what married people do. There is now perhaps a universal awareness that the basic rules of the family game are being challenged, rather than individuals cheating in terms of rules that themselves are dependable. The relationship between husband and wife, and in different ways between parent and child, is being looked at critically by people who are aware that neither the law nor any other institution of society has, in reality, the power to compel within the home behavior that people do not believe in.

Let us take a quick historical look at what marriage meant, then proceed to some of the forces of change today, after which we can say a few things about what may happen to marriage within the next generation. Two major principles underlying our model of marriage in 1990 emerge. They are: (a) freedom to personally and explicitly contract the type of marriage one wishes; and (b) formal public or communal control over parenthood.

Much of today's family law comes rather directly from canon law, which is based on the Judaeo-Christian scriptures. Canon law is still with us, for instance, in forbidding spouses with whom a relationship would be considered incestuous; also, the flavor of the canon law remains in recognizing adultery as the major grounds for divorce, thus the gravest crime to commit against the spouse.

What does it mean, in a behavioral sense, to consider marriage a "sacrament" rather than a secular contract? Essentially, seeing marriage as a religious arrangement is connected with various beliefs about an afterlife as well as fears of divine retribution which may occur in the present existence or in an afterlife. People will, whether they are enjoying themselves or not, avoid doing certain things in their married life (as in other spheres of behavior) if they fear heavenly displeasure.

However, the idea that marriage will be considered a sacrament by people who have given up religion as an effective force in their daily lives in every other sphere does not make sense. We may say that the canon law approach which underlies family law in general is now obsolete, because the expectations that people have of themselves and of each other which depend on supernatural sanction do not hold and the traditional image of the family no longer works. Why?

Secularization, which for our purposes may mean simply the decline of religious thinking as an influence on one's day-to-day decision-making, has meant that the only sanctions that would really work within the home (where neither police nor judges can observe one's behavior) have been effectively destroyed. Once this belief in religious, supernatural justice is gone, the sacredness of marriage becomes a legal fiction or historical relic, rather than a description of the way marriage is currently viewed subjectively and the way behavior will really occur.

Furthermore, urbanization and mobility have led to the ending of other sanctions that were very important in maintaining traditional marriage.

The trend is toward decline of informal, personal social control over married couples which was formerly exercised by kinsmen and neighbors. It would not make sense to anticipate massive changes in the law and explicit contractual entry into marriage as the normal way to shape married life, if mate selection and the interactions between husband and wife were still under the regulation of custom, vigilantly enforced by aunts, grandfathers or brothers-in-law. It is precisely because the vast mobility of modern living has led, along with other factors, to the isolation of the nuclear family—the source of so many problems in the family sphere today—that this new kind of regulation will be called into force and accepted as necessary and proper.

Thirdly, coeducation and employment of women have led to the destruction of male family "headship," since male supremacy can hardly exist without women being, of necessity, dependent upon husbands and therefore disposed "for their own benefit" to go along with his instructions.

All of this means that both men and women are able to really make their own choices in marriage, free from (a) fears of supernatural judgment, (b) judgment by the immediately relevant community, and at the same time wives have less and less reason to listen to their husbands if what the husband says is not particularly agreeable. It is not some abstract cultural or ideological shift which has brought about the tremendous variability and freedom that we find in modern marriage, but these reality factors.

In most countries of the West, except possibly Sweden and a few other Scandinavian countries, family law implies the patriarchal model of marriage: He works and decides, she stays at home and cooks. These premises may be less and less true, but until very recently they were not challenged as an image of the "typical" marriage and a definition of its "normal" form. More and more people are realizing that these premises are not true, and perhaps not worth making true after the fact.

Now the law throughout North America still provides for easy and quick marriage, but hard and slow divorce. There seems to be a terrible imbalance if entry into this state, which involves so many decisions and problems, is made deceptively facile while exit from it is made extremely difficult. Of course, one important reason for such a difference is that at the time of marriage there are no children's rights to think of (although there are quite a few marriages nowadays where children either have come into the world already or have been conceived) while divorce is often a situation where the rights of children have to be considered.

But, this does not justify, in my thinking, such a difference between the contracting of a marriage and one's terminating such a relationship. We cannot assume that forcing an unhappy couple to stay together, in an "empty-shell" marriage, constitutes a good environment for their children! This emphasis, too, is a remnant of the canon law influence on family law in general, since traditionally the Christian view was that marriage is important and universal but divorce is not to be accepted.

Perhaps it will be possible to reduce the "legal lag" between what the law says and what people are doing, in future. It is likely that such reforming and correlation is going to be speeded up in the next few decades, so that the extent to which there is an uncomfortable and problematic contradiction between the law in force and what people are really doing will be virtually eliminated.

Thus, all of the ongoing changes with regard to contraception, abortion, new types of marriage contract, etc., will—it is here assumed —be accepted and in a sense ratified by the law, as the old-style moralists who can still be found in our agencies of social control cease to fight a rear-guard action against the new norms that are, whether they like them or not, emerging.

It must be remembered that there will remain in the foreseeable future, a traditionalist minority even in the most advanced and change-prone societies. This segment will expend much effort to maintain patterns of marriage and family living that they feel are right, and which are consistent with the patterns they experienced when they were children. This traditionalist minority will certainly not be gone, or reduced to insignificant numbers, in the short span of one generation; therefore, any predictions we make must take into account not only what the "new wave" pattern is going to be, but also the fact that there will be a considerable number of people who elect to maintain the familiar value system that they were socialized with, and to which they are deeply committed.

What may be on its way for marriage in about 20 years? First, we can assume that courtship will, as it does currently, serve as a testing ground for the kind of marriage that people have in their minds, perhaps even dimly or unconsciously. Thus, insofar as particular young men or women may have begun to feel that the type of marriage they would like is Type A rather than Type B, their courtship would be of the sort that normally leads to Type A, and in a sense tests their readiness to build their relationship along those lines.

An important consequence of widespread social-science knowledge among young people today, which is coupled with a greater use of principles drawn from sociology and anthropology in the process of law reform, will be the recognition that continuity or consistency for each person or married couple is necessary, in regard to the larger questions at least, for a particular marriage system to work well in the long run.

Of course, courtship will serve this testing and assessing function after people have been approximately matched through computer mate-finding methods. Random dating and hopeless courtships will have been largely prevented through the provision of basic categoric information which people can use to screen possible spouses, such as total years of schooling completed, aptitude and IQ scores, major subjects (which are related to intellectual interests in a very direct way), religiosity, leisure and recreation preferences, and similar things.

For remarriage suitors, data on wealth or credit and occupation would also be used, along with some indication of attitudes concerning home life and procreation. Since homogamy (similarity between spouses) is recognized as an important indicator of marital success, such information will be systematically gathered and made available to cut down on the wasteful chance element in mate selection. It is only when people are continuing their search for a spouse within the appropriate "pool," at a mutually right point, that courtship as a series of informal but direct experiments in relationship-building will come into play.

For couples who do not intend to engage in parenthood, and

therefore have a right to exercise their own freedom as private persons, we can expect that today's yes-or-no marriage choice will be replaced by a much more individualized freedom of contract, in which couples will enter that kind of marriage which suits them. This could be done either by offering different kinds of marriage from which each couple will select one (at a time), to which they are then bound, or by engaging the services of a marrying counselor (likely a lawyer) who would assist couples in drawing up their own internally consistent contracts.

Neither monogamy nor indefinite permanence are important in this respect, so they will not be required. However, the agreed-upon choice will be explicit and recorded so there's no question of deception or misunderstanding, as well as to provide statistical information, and official registration of this choice is an element of marriage which will remain a matter of public concern.

Explicit choice of the kind of marriage one enters into is, of course, an effect not only of the emancipation of women, but of men as well. What will some of the major options be? With the insurance functions that were formerly secured by having children (who would provide during one's old age) being completely taken over by the government (assisted by unions, pension funds and the like), there will be little reason to warn those who choose childlessness against this course.

With celibacy no bar to sexual satisfaction (because of the acceptance of nonmarital sex with contraceptives), society will accept the idea that some segments of the population can obtain whatever intimate satisfactions they require in a series of casual, short-term "affairs" (as we call them today), and will never enter any publicly registered marriage.

Another not-unfamiliar option in this regard will be the renewable trial marriage, in which people explicitly contract for a childless union which is to be comprehensively evaluated after three years or five years, at which point either a completely new decision can be reached or the same arrangement can be renewed for another term of three or five years.

This would not be, then, a question of divorce; it is simply a matter of a definite arrangement having expired. The contract having been for a limited term, both parties are perfectly free to decide not to renew it when that term is over. This would be a normal, perhaps minor, part of one's "marital career."

A third option, which introduces very few complications, is the permanent childless marriage; the arrangement between the two adults is of indefinite duration, but they have agreed in advance that there will be no offspring, and of course, there is no question but that medical technology will make it possible for them to live up to that part of the arrangement. Some will choose sterilization, others will use contraceptive methods which can be abandoned if one changes his mind and is authorized to procreate.

Compound marriages will also be allowed whether they be polygamous, polyandrous or group marriages. However, these communes will not be free of the same obligations that any marriage entails, such as formally registering the terms of the agreement among the members; any significant change in the arrangements among members of such a familial commune will have to be recorded in the appropriate public place in the same way as marriages and divorces which involve only one husband and one wife.

There will be great freedom with regard to the number of people in the commune, but internal consistency concerning the give-and-take among the members, their privileges and obligations, will be required. The functional, pragmatic ethic emerging in today's youth culture will be strictly adhered to, some years hence, not as moral absolutes, not because people have come to the belief that these represent the true right and wrong, but in order to prevent serious conflict.

With the majority of young people in society choosing one of the foregoing patterns, the number of marriages in which children are expected will be relatively small; perhaps 25 to 30 percent of the population will be so serious about having children that they will be prepared to undergo the rigorous training and careful evaluation necessary for them to obtain the requisite licenses.

The marriages intended to produce children will usually be classic familistic marriages, in which the general pattern of interaction between husband and wife, as well as the relationship between parent and child, may be fairly similar to the contemporary upper middle class marriage of today's society that have the best socio-emotional climate. The community will be assured that this home atmosphere is, in fact, most probable, since it has been prepared for, rather than left to an accident of kind fate and to happenstance talents that people bring to parenthood nowadays.

All those who desire to become parents, and therefore to exercise a public responsibility in an extremely important and sensitive area of personal functioning, will have to prove that they are indeed the right people to serve as society's agents of socialization. Just as those who wish to adopt a child, nowadays, are subjected to intensive interviewing which aims at discovering the healthiness of the relationship between husband and wife and of the motivation for parenthood, the suitability that the man or woman displays for coping with the stresses of parenthood, as well as the physical and material conditions that the adopted child will be enjoying, the evaluation of mother and father applicants in future will be done by a team of professionals who have to reach the judgment that this particular individual or couple have the background to become professionals themselves, that is, recognized and certified parents.

We can expect whatever else happens, that scientific family life education will become a standard part of the curriculum (at least in public high schools) so that almost everyone will have some systematic awareness of the issues in married life and the problems that they are likely to confront.

The course of study for parenthood will include such subjects as: human reproduction and gestation; infant care; developmental physiology and psychology; theories of socialization; and educational psychology. Starting with a foundation of systematic but abstract scientific knowledge, the practical and applied course in hygienic, nutritional, emotional and perceptual-aesthetic care of children will follow, in the same way as training for medicine and other professions. In addition, prospective parents will be required to achieve some clarity concerning values and philosophy of life, in which they will be guided by humanistic scholars, and will also be required to attain a clear understanding of the mass media, their impact on children, and how to manage mass media consumption as an important part of socialization in the modern urban environment.

One side effect of such parent training may be a sharp drop in the power of the peer group, as parents do more with greater self-confidence.

Suitable examinations will be devised, and only those who achieve adequate grades in these areas will be given a parenthood license.

Some young men and women are likely to take parenthood curriculum "just in case": that is, although they have not yet thought through the type of marriage that they desire or the kind of spouse they are looking for, they may continue their education by entering parenthood studies and obtaining the diploma, should it turn out that they elect a classic, child-rearing marriage later on. Possibly, fathers will be prohibited from full-time employment outside the home while they have preschool children, or if their children have extra needs shown by poor conduct or other symptoms of psychic distress.

The right of society to control parenthood is something that can be predicted from a number of things we already know. For one thing, the rising incidence of battered and neglected children, and our almost total inability to really cope with the battered child's problem except after the fact, will certainly lead legislators to planning how those people who can be discovered, in advance, to be unfit for parenthood may be screened out and prevented from begetting offspring who will be the wretched target of their parents' emotional inadequacies.

Furthermore, increasing awareness of the early childhood roots of serious crime and delinquency will also lead to an attempt to prevent major deviance by seeing to it that early socialization occurs under favorable circumstances. It does not appear that there will be many other really effective ways in which rising crime rates could eventually be reversed.

This, however, will again mean that those who raise children will have to be evaluated for this purpose in some way, by society and the open community.

If such testing and selection is not done, we have no way to protect ourselves from large numbers of young people who have been raised in a way that almost inevitably will have them providing the murderers, rapists and robbers of the next generation. Since we now begin to have the technology and the knowledge to prevent this, we may confidently expect that parent-licensing is going to come into force soon [cf.: McIntire, p. 94].

This picture of the marriage situation in 1990 leaves open various questions and problems. One of the difficulties in this scenario is the question of what authority will make the necessary decision: What sorts of committees will be in charge of devising the various internally consistent kinds of marriage, working out the parent education courses, and certifying people for parenthood? There are, after all, political implications to controlling marriage and parenthood in this way, and the general public will have to be satisfied that those who exercise authority in this area are, in fact, competent as well as impartial.

Another problem is that of securing complete and valid information: (a) for those preparing to locate suitable mates through computer matching, or to make a commitment in some specific form of marriage; and (b) concerning those who apply for the parenthood course and later for the license to practice parenthood.

Unless we can be sure that the inputs used for making such judgments contain information which is adequate in quantity and true as well, these new systems will not be able to function without a great deal of deviance, and might easily engender problems which are worse than those today.

A third issue is that of parenthood having tied people to the community. What will childlessness do to one's motivation for planning/preserving; will it demotivate all long-range investment? Research on this could start now, comparing parents with the childless.

The great misery of many families today makes it evident enough that radical change is needed. The law will have to catch up with most of society—educated youth, the affluent classes, liberated women, and the culture of poverty. All these are starting to experience new family norms of which the law gives no hint.

Chapter 8

toward a more flexible monogamy

Raymond J. Lawrence

The time has come to begin a serious public conversation about the validity of the popular and traditional notions of marriage. Permanence and sexual exclusiveness have for generations been the hallmark of the institution of marriage. However, the permanence of marriage has been challenged openly and publicly in recent decades, as evidenced by the escalating divorce rate. What has been called serial polygamy is in wide public practice. The aura of shame that in the past surrounded divorce and remarriage is evaporating rapidly. The Episcopal church, for example, signaled this public trend in its 1973 national convention by making it easier for divorced Episcopalians to remarry. Even the staunch position of Roman Catholics against divorce and remarriage is yielding to the practicalities of daily life and new theological insights.

If the permanence of marriage is eroding, so is the sexual exclusiveness of marriage. Rustum and Della Roy, in their book *Honest Sex,* pioneered the contemporary challenge to exclusiveness in marriage. More recently, Morton Hunt in *The Affair* and the writings of Gerhard Neubeck and Robert and Anna Francoeur have continued this trend. Robert Rimmer, best known through *The Harrad Experiment,* has undertaken in his novels something of a personal crusade against the exclusiveness of marriage. There are many others. My own marriage counseling experience supports the broad thrust of these writings, namely that some married couples seem to create an intimate and satisfactory marital relationship without the traditional exclusiveness of the marriage contract's "forsaking all others."

"Toward a More Flexible Monogamy" by Raymond J. Lawrence. This article appears by permission of the author.

My own theoretical bias is that the permanence of marriage is to be more greatly valued than exclusiveness. This bias runs counter to popular wisdom, which generally attaches more shame to an affair than to a separation. My clinical impressions from years of working professionally with troubled marriages is that persons with non-exclusive marriages generally do better than persons who choose a life of serial polygamy. An affair brings people together. Divorce separates. In the long run it is better that people come together, though for certain reasons separation is valuable too. It is my conclusion that for some couples the permanence of their relationship can be enhanced by relaxing the exclusive character of their relationship.

Culturally speaking, there is no denying the trouble marriage is in. It is an institution that has been asked to carry more weight than it can bear. Persons are reared to expect that a traditional marriage will satisfy all their needs for deep intimacy in human relationships. But these expectations do not seem to be met in the vast majority of the marriages to which I have had opportunity to give consultation. Furthermore, the prime values of traditional marriage are security and predictability. But we are living at a time in which new and different values are being discovered, such as spontaneity, sensory awareness, and the stimulation and variety of multiple, intimate human relationships. For example, Charles A. Reich, in his widely read *The Greening of America,* advocates sex "experience with many different people, in different times, circumstances, and localities, in moments of happiness, sorrow, need, and comfortable familiarity, in youth and in age." In the eyes of many persons today, the security and predictability which traditional marriage provides do not compare favorably with the values of stimulation and variety that can be achieved through multiple intimate human relationships.

So we are living in a time when alternatives to traditional monogamy are shaping up. For better or for worse, it is clear that increasing numbers of persons are deciding that an exclusive sexual relationship with one other person through a lifetime is an unnecessary ascetic commitment. The most prevalent pattern of response to this discovery is the increasing practice of what has been called serial polygamy, which is the contracting of one marriage after another. In serial polygamy one's needs for the stimulation and variety of multiple human relationships can be met. But what is lost in serial polygamy is the value of a continuing, lifelong relationship. And for many persons this too is a value well worth preserving.

There is a new form of marriage in the making today which attempts to bring together the values of both traditional monogamy and polygamy. It is an attempt to hold to both the value of lifelong commitment between two persons and the value of the stimulation that can come from the variety of multiple intimate relationships. Dr. Robert Francoeur of Fairleigh Dickinson University and Anna Francoeur suggest that this new form of marriage be called *Flexible Monogamy*. They suggest this label as a description of a marriage in which a lifelong commitment is integrated with a variety of satellite relationships. Other names have also been suggested for this new form of marriage. Rustum and Della Roy, for instance, refer in their writings to marriages which permit "comarital relationships." Nena and George O'Neill have dealt in depth with the contrast between what they call a traditional, closed marriage and the new pattern of open marriage. As the Francoeurs explore them elsewhere in this anthology, the similarities between these three models is striking.

On one level, Flexible Monogamy is not new. Extramarital sex, or the affair, is certainly as old as marriage. When I began my career as a clergyman fourteen years ago, the most startling task which faced me and the one for which I felt least prepared in my training, was the task of working with married persons who were struggling with the problem of extramarital relationships. Though extramarital sex is not new, what is new is the increasing evidence that extramarital sex may well be openly and contractually integrated into a marriage with creative and positive results. So integrated, extramarital sex becomes both legitimized and, at the same time, made less threatening to the marriage itself. What makes it less threatening is that it holds a subordinate position to the primary pair-bond relationship of the marriage. A "satellite" relationship is inherently a subordinate relationship. I assume that the wives of the Old Testament patriarchs, for example, were far less disturbed about their husbands' concubines than the average wife is about her husband's lover. Concubines were, of course, legitimized, but in a subordinate or satellite position.

Flexible Monogamy is different from traditional monogamy on one main issue. Traditional monogamy is an *exclusive,* genital sexual relationship. Flexible Monogamy is a *primary but nonexclusive,* genital sexual relationship. Exclusive relationships do have advantages. They provide a measure of security and predictability which cannot be achieved any other way. But in order to maintain security and predictability, one must sacrifice the stimulation of the new. A primary relationship, as opposed to an exclusive relationship, is one in which two persons give to each other their first loyalty, while permitting each other the relative freedom to search and explore other relationships, even to the point of genital sexual intimacy.

Within traditional monogamy, extramarital sex is usually experienced as a bid to supplant the existing marriage with a new one. Statistically, it does not generally happen that an affair which disrupts a marriage develops into a subsequent marriage. But the threat of being supplanted is nevertheless what is often experienced. A relationship which is contracted itself to be total or exclusive cannot by definition incorporate the competition even of a minor satellite. It must remain total or be disrupted. I have heard many a spouse complain that his marriage partner could not tolerate gracefully any form of appreciation of another person of the opposite sex. Such are often the fruits of an exclusive contract. On the other hand, a marriage contract which espouses a primary loyalty rather than an exclusive allegiance will permit minor competition, or a satellite relationship, so long as the primacy of the original relationship is kept intact. A flexible monogamy allows for satellite sexual relationships, and these relationships may or may not include full genital intimacy.

As a clergyman who specializes in marriage counseling, I have known of numerous examples of extramarital affairs which have been largely destructive in their intent and many which have been largely destructive in their results as well. I have known women who got themselves pregnant in an affair in order to take revenge against their husbands. I have known of men who sought to estrange their lovers from their husbands for no other purpose than to prove to themselves their own masculine prowess. I have known of persons who "accidentally" get themselves discovered in an affair as a way of communicating something with forceful hostility to their spouses. But much has been written already by therapists and ministers about the ways in which extramarital sex is used as a destructive device in human relationships.

These are some of the pitfalls of extramarital sex. The implication, of course, is that the entire territory is evil, but there is evidence that this may no longer be the case. It is time to reexamine the whole question of extramarital relations.

THE AFFAIR AS A FAITHFUL ACTIVITY

An affair which is engaged in for an ulterior purpose is an unfaithful act. For example, an affair which gives the participant the pleasure of having "done something to one's spouse," whether or not he or she becomes aware of it, is an unfaithful act. It is a human relationship engaged in, not for its own sake, but for the ulterior purpose of doing something to a third party. An activity which has an ulterior purpose is not an authentic activity in its own right. For example, the person who goes from one relationship to another to reassure himself of his powers to attract other persons is hardly faithful to the relationships he creates. He does not become involved with another for the sake of communicating and relating intimately to another, and therefore he is not faithful to the relationship. He merely satisfies the ulterior purpose of enhancing his own feelings of potency and power. A faithful affair is one engaged in for its own sake, where one seeks primarily neither to hurt nor to please any other person, and where the only significant agenda is the intimate participation in the being of another person.

THE LONGING FOR INNOCENCE AND THE FAILURE TO ACHIEVE AUTONOMY

Just as the decision in favor of an affair may be made for inappropriate or unwise reasons, so the refusal of an affair may be likewise for inappropriate or unwise reasons. Many persons avoid an affair because of a desire for innocence or because of extreme dependency feelings, and a failure to achieve autonomy. These attitudes are appropriate to young children. And, obviously, many adults remain children in their psychosexual development. Such persons, whether they are "good" or "bad," perform in relation to their parents, or their parent ego state—the introjected parent. They may have an affair in order to perform as a "bad child," or they may refuse an affair in order to perform as a "good child," or vice versa. In any instance, their behavior is immature, not because of the act or because of the refusal to act, but because of the basis on which their decision is made.

1. The Longing for Innocence

The need to feel innocent may be the most underestimated intrapersonal dynamic in the arena of human relationships. Relatively immature persons need to feel relatively innocent, in direct proportion to their lack of maturity. The process of fulfilling one's sexual potential is a continuing story of the loss of innocence. When the adolescent masturbates for the first time, he loses a feeling of innocence. I recall an adolescent boy, Roger by name, who felt the necessity of confessing to his parents his acts of masturbation. His parents, who were rather sophisticated and highly educated people, at first thought this was a commendable gesture on his part. But, in fact, his confession was dynamically a regressive and not a very promising development. Roger's confession was a striving to regain his lost innocence in relation to his parents and the parental world. It was a step backwards in his psychosexual development. Masturbation is hardly an activity for which one can appropriately expect to obtain genuine parental approval, and yet it is an experience which probably everyone needs to have. In my counseling with Roger my intention was to help him develop more independence, or even an interim counter-dependence. My hope was that he become autonomous enough to bear his own guilt feelings rather than to take flight to a childlike innocence. Though it is appropriate to children, innocence is not the highest form of human life. The more spiritually mature one is, the more he is capable of embracing a measure of alien elements, such as guilt or the loss of innocence.

The meaning of the Judaic and Christian symbols of the forgiveness of sins is that man need no longer bear the burden of the necessity to be innocent. The fact that many persons in the Judaic and Christian religious groups take these symbols as a call to return to innocence is irrelevant. In reality, the forgiveness of sins is not a call back to childish innocence, but rather a call toward a maturity or manliness that is capable of embracing the loss of one's innocence.[1]

Many married persons find themselves struggling with their own sexuality in ways similar to Roger and his struggle with his masturbation. I have met significant numbers of persons for whom the principal deterrent to an affair is the overriding need to feel innocent. What is surprising to me is the frequency with which this dynamic is at work in a marriage even when the other spouse has already revealed an affair. The need to feel innocent, then, is not necessarily lessened by the revealed "guilt" of one's spouse. Quite frequently I have met a husband or wife who quite sincerely, but secretly, wished his or her spouse would have an affair in order to reset a balance of power, or in order to equalize the relationship. But there are few interpersonal problems more difficult to work through to resolution than the negotiation between an "innocent" and a "guilty" partner in a troubled marriage. The clinging to innocence may be childishness. But "innocent" persons cling to their supposed virtue with great tenacity.

The need to feel innocent often creates another very common problem. It is quite frequently the underlying dynamic that compels persons abruptly to confess to their spouses their sexual adventures. A typical pattern following an abrupt confession to one's spouse is that the one who confesses becomes the target of anger, hostility, and/or shame. He may then experience his punishment and as a result feel cleansed and, in a sense, restored to innocence. This is a neurotic pattern. The neurosis derives from the failure to experience enough grace and forgiveness in life to enable one to tolerate his forever lost innocence. A man may choose to suffer and perhaps even to

1 As Dr. Michael Valente points out in his book, *Sex: The Radical View of a Catholic Theologian,* the sacrament of Penance is not a magical ritual of soul cleansing but a conviction of faith on the part of the believer that, although he is a sinner who has lost his innocence, he is nevertheless justified and saved by the merits of Jesus.

die in order to pay for his loss of innocence. Or he may find at the heart of life enough grace and forgiveness to have his brokenness forgiven and blessed. In this world, the fall of man (Adam) is a fall upward. The land east of Eden when man lives may be full of sorrow and toil. But joys are to be found there too. And what man would return to the land of innocence? A sign of the spiritually mature man is that he no longer need pay for his loss of innocence. Such a man is the second Adam, the new man. It is to this that man is called.

2. The Failure to Achieve Autonomy

A common fallacy in marriage folklore is that real intimacy means full disclosure of one's thoughts, feelings, and actions. I contend that an attempt at total openness is not a true form of intimacy. It is rather a naïve form of dependency. Real intimacy is experienced in the rhythmical movement toward and away from another person. Real intimacy is experienced only when persons have the capacity and wisdom both to give and to withhold, both to move toward and to move away from, both to be close and to be distant. One who cannot be distant destroys the value of his being close. One who cannot be close negates the value of his distance.

So in marriage persons need to find a rhythm of closeness and distance in their relationship. I have met many persons who ask their spouses for something that sounds like total openness. Total openness is an oppressive and smothering goal toward which to work. The fact is that most marriages need both more closeness and more distance, each in its own time, following whatever rhythm a particular couple may develop for themselves.

One of the dynamics of persons who have affairs is that they are no longer in the position of being able to "tell all." Full disclosure to one's spouse becomes much more problematic than among the traditionally monogamous. A satellite relationship does not lend itself to supper-table conversation or pillow talk with one's spouse. I have found it to be almost invariably true that married persons do not want to hear any of the details of the exploits of their spouses with a third party. An unusually articulate counselee of mine put it this way:

> Just before Jackie and I were married, I told her about all the sexual experiences I had had before I met her. Of course I was young then and there wasn't a lot to tell, but I somehow felt like I owed it to her to tell her everything. It was a sort of cleaning the slate between her and me. It kind of surprised me several years later when I found out from her that these revelations made her angry . . . Now in the past year, after having gotten involved with Barbara, I still sometimes feel the need of telling Jackie everything. It's sort of like I want her

to know everything I have done. I am not sure whether this is because I am seeking her approval or whether I simply want to share with her everything that is important to me. Perhaps both. But since I have been talking to you, I think I have finally discovered it is okay to have secrets. The fact is, I now think secrets are necessary to my being a man. It is like they are part of my manhood. And I think to tell her everything is sort of like treating her as if she is my mother.

One of the limitations of an affair is that the joy of it does not lend itself to sharing with one's spouse.

An inhibiting dynamic to extramarital sex for many persons, then, lies in the distaste for the distance or the withholding that is necessary in relation to one's spouse. Of course, it goes without saying that these same persons likely lack genuine intimacy in their marriages as well. In fact, it is certainly true that a significant number of marriages today could be described as mutually oppressive and clinging dependency relationships. A counselee of mine, a male school teacher, was complaining that he was becoming impotent with his wife. He had recently lost his ability to maintain an erection. In the course of our conversation it emerged that he had developed some very deep feelings for a colleague of his on the teaching faculty. He had never so much as touched his new friend physically, but nevertheless his conflicted feelings were quite powerful. He felt terribly guilty for even having such feelings, and guilt rose up within him when he was in the presence of his wife, particularly when they were about to have sexual intercourse. What this person illustrates is a rather extreme example of clinging dependency, the failure to achieve a significant degree of autonomy in relation to one's spouse.

Conclusion

I am favorably impressed with the shape of the contract that many couples have made for themselves. I am also often favorably impressed with the quality of their relationships. The evidence of respect and love they have for each other is very substantial. Although there seems to be a high degree of intimacy in their relationships, there is a relative absence of possessiveness and clinging dependency that characterizes so many marriages. Their marriages are no longer an exclusive relationship, though there is a strong primary loyalty to each other. And this loyalty is the cornerstone of their marriages. They have chosen an unorthodox form of marriage to be sure. Those who think that orthodox patterns of life are entirely adequate for everyone who attempts to live fully in these days will find this flexible monogamy a spurious venture. But it is my hunch that the unorthodoxy of Open Marriage or Flexible Monogamy will be for some persons a harbinger of a more satisfactory way of understanding marriage in the years ahead.

I suggest that a new form of marriage is in the making that increasing numbers of persons are likely to contract for themselves. Whether it is called Flexible Monogamy, Open Marriage, or something else is of little importance. The shape of the contract is more important than the label put on it.

It is evident that something serious is happening to the institution of marriage today. Traditional monogamy has lost its credibility as the only way for heterosexual social organization. It is by no means about to disappear from the cultural landscape, but it will most certainly have to compete in the years ahead with other forms of marriage. The challenge that faces clergymen and others who give counsel to persons struggling with the issues of human existence is that of evaluating with an open mind this emergent pattern of life. It is simple enough to parrot the orthodoxy of the past. It is a more complex task to struggle with the present and to attempt to test the value of new and unanticipated social phenomena.

PART FOUR

the future
of parenthood

If the American and European model of marriage has tied love and marriage together "like horse and carriage," so too have we made parenthood a necessary component of all marriages. But the harness between marriage and parenthood is fast wearing thin. In a *U. S. News & World Report* article[1] some statistics testified to this dissolution. One wife out of every twenty-five between the ages of eighteen and twenty-four wanted no children at all, and ten percent of all young married couples wanted only one child. One out of four college students in Stockton, California want no children when they marry. The trend in the last decade had definitely been toward smaller families and childless marriages both in reality and in expectation.

In this section we will look at several aspects of parenthood in the decade or two ahead: the decline of motherhood and its social, economic, and psychological impact, the single person as a parent and the licensing of parenthood.

Fire a few hundred workers from their jobs, and the political, economic, and social reaction will be hard to ignore locally. Compare that reaction with the consequences we face today as our contraceptive

[1] *U. S. News & World Report.* "Is the American Family in Danger?" April 16, 1973, p. 71 ff.

75

technology, longer life-spans, reduced infant mortality, and the economic liberation of women threaten a billion or more women with the loss of their traditional, socially vital, eighteen-hour-a-day jobs which filled their whole adult life with meaning. These jobs gave women a kind of status in a man's world, even when all other avenues to status failed or were ruled out for females.

"Every occupational group fights for survival when threatened with technological obsolescence and tries to retain a monopoly over its technical skills," sociologist Jeanne Binstock reminds us. And women —mothers—are no exception. Threatened with loss of their career, mothers become overly possessive, supervisors of every childish, trivial activity and thought, using guilt to bind their few children to them in life-long, dependent need. But the overinjection of guilt turns young people against the capitalistic system which demands competition and aggression, and against the Protestant work ethic. The consequences of motherhood's decline, as Binstock outlines these, will be *revolutionary*, to use an abused but very appropriate adjective.

For centuries, our whole social and economic structure has been geared to monogamy and the two-parent family. For adults this has been the sole pattern acceptable to society, though spinster aunts and the occasional nomad bachelor were tolerated on the fringes of the adult world. It has been a functional pattern and certainly a major factor in the triumph of Western capitalism and our industrial society. With women providing an essential domestic support system, taking care of the children and providing a nest-refuge for the husband, the male was free to devote a full day's energies to gainful employment outside the home.

But the past century has also witnessed two critical changes in this environment, noted earlier by Robert Francoeur: an increasing acceptance of divorce, plus an ever earlier sexual maturity coupled with ever later marriages. The once-rare divorced parent and the occasional widow or widower who quickly remarried has been replaced by the divorced parent who swears "never again" or is very cautious about getting remarried, by the widowed who are less pressured by family and friends to remarry immediately, and by the single person, male or female, who decides to raise a family without a spouse. Today, single men and women can adopt children, even if they are self-acknowledged homosexuals or lesbians.

In the decade of the '60s, the single adult population of the United States rose from twenty-nine million to forty-nine million. In less than a decade, from 1965 to 1973, the number of single parent families has risen by 31.4 percent, nearly triple the increase in standard two-parent families. The consequences of this parallel trend are bound to be far-reaching. As a society, we will have to find a replacement for the domestic support system once provided by the wife-house-keeper-mother. Economically, in our tax structures, we will have to work toward a more equitable balance in burdens. Legally, the rights of the single person will have to be protected against discrimination. The new adult life-styles of the single person and the single parent will need a functional support system which the following review from the *U. S. News & World Report* highlights in terms of hard practicalities.

Until recently, few, if any, questions have been raised about the "inalienable" right we have always allowed every sexually mature adult, provided they obtained a license to share another person's bed.

University of Maryland psychologist Roger McIntire uses a not-so-futuristic scenario to focus on the advantages of a society legally controlling parenthood. He raises the distinct possibility that we or our children may sooner or later decide to restrict parenting to adults who qualify by training and testing for the most demanding of all careers.

We might even go beyond McIntire's suggestion, radical as it is, and ask whether with the liberation of women from the nursery and kitchen, with their growing economic and psychological independence, some not-so-future generation may find itself with a majority of women unwilling to bear the discomfort, inconveniences, and associated physical disabilities of pregnancy. If males were able to bear children, how many would gladly embrace a fetus for nine months? Should we go beyond McIntire's very sensitive alternatives and consider whether some future generation may not have to offer considerable benefits to induce women to bear children?

Chapter 9

motherhood: an occupation facing decline

Jeanne Binstock

Twenty years from now, mothers will be a mere specialty group in the United States. This state of affairs will not result from the women's liberation movement, but from economic factors and technological change.

The U.S. now is going through a momentous and rapid occupational shift, recalling the movement of peasants into factories during the Industrial Revolution. The new occupational trend is a response to both past-push (the atrophy of one set of specialized functions) and future-pull (the emergence of a new set of specialized functions). U.S. efforts to accomplish this necessary economic transformation will provide a model for other nations reaching a post-industrial state of development.

Modern medicine's success in reducing mortality has resulted in an overproduction of people. Effective mass contraception offers a remedy for the problem. Women's lib movements are really a consequence of technological change; they have appeared at the historical moment when a sharp reduction in the occupational group known as mothers is mandatory, and the technological capacity to achieve it is available. In understanding what is happening, it is important to bear in mind that ideological change can occur only when the technological capacities for achieving it are available. Just as the Protestant Ethic lubricated the spread of capitalism, so the women's lib ideology will lubricate the necessary occupational shift of masses of mothers into the emerging new society.

"Motherhood: An Occupation Facing Decline" by Jeanne Binstock. From *The Futurist*, published by the World Future Society, P.O. Box 30369, Bethesda Branch, Washington, D.C. 20014.

But before we consider the future, let us look at the more recent past and the present.

Mothers have traditionally been the world's largest occupational group. Half the population was assigned to a single task—producing people, with all the resulting obligations of child care. The huge allocation of human resources was absolutely necessary to maintain an adequate adult population in the face of war and disease, and it was a logical assignment of roles. After all, what else could any group of people do if they were almost always pregnant, or physically incapacitated as they recuperated from one delivery or awaited the next, or in danger of dying every 18 months, or needed to be constantly available for feeding children. The job title was Mother, and, just as in other occupational groups, the job was invested with an occupational mystique, a jargon, a particular life-style, and some specialized technical skills.

MOTHERHOOD MUST FALL INTO DISREPUTE

The consequences of modern medicine have caught us off guard, and we are forced to face the fact that if we do not take from women their role of mother and replace it with something else, we will be throttled by the overproduction of babies. We thus face the need to demand that the ancient and honorable occupation of motherhood fall into disrepute, and that women commit themselves to other occupations. Women must be "liberated" to enjoy the fruits of other occupations, *whether they want to be or not.*

Many things must change in the next 10 years, because most women—not just a few—have access to cheap and effective means of contraception and because the survival chances of most children, rather than an elite few, have been drastically improved by readily available medical care. Motherhood must undergo a drastic revision.

The coming revolution in motherhood will not, however, be the first metamorphosis due to technological change. The 19th-century industrial revolution produced an important but largely unnoticed change in the mother's role. When machine processes took men away from the home, the socialization of children was left to the women, who had previously acted only with authority delegated by men. With their physical superiority and economic power in the family, men have always relied on force or the threat of it. They mold and shape by fear. Women, lacking economic power, status, or physical force, have had no option but to socialize by motivational seduction (persuasion) and by guilt. When women took over the socialization of children, the process was transformed from manipulation by threat of force to manipulation by seduction, enticement, and guilt. Brutal physical punishment—and even spanking and slapping—have become almost extinct among the middle classes; indeed, by 18th century standards, physical punishment is almost extinct in the western world. Mothers today shape the development of the child by assuming love and trust in the products of her body and demanding guilt. The changed style of child-rearing has had specific consequences for the character formation of people in the highly industrialized countries. The emphasis has shifted from external behavior to internal motives.

The socialization of children is becoming increasingly manipulatory, seductive (in the psychological sense), and oriented toward guilt, that is to say, toward psychic rather than physical punishment. In the U.S. and a few European nations during the past 30 years, the attenuation of motherhood as an occupation—due to reduced infant mortality and middle-class contraception—has led to more pervasive and intensive guilt, not only as a socialization device but as a way of life.

In the past, mothers often had to fight to stay alive after childbirth and to keep their children alive. Children required continual nursing during bouts of critical illness and often died, causing a grief hard to assuage even by the birth of the next child (often already on the way). Today many an American woman has never exhausted herself from childbirth and the fear of childbirth, has never sat up night after night with a child screaming in pain, and has never wondered if the astonishing fruit of her body would remain alive to adulthood. Instead of endurance, patience, fortitude, and tenderness— the traditional virtues of women in all previous historical periods— we have contraception and penicillin.

Today the American woman has two or three children, instead of six or eight; childbirth for her is not a battle for survival; she is rarely up at night with a sick child; she has plenty of household appliances, processed foods and other technological innovations that function as para-mothers. In addition, specialized agencies such as schools, clubs, and television share her burdens. She has succumbed, half willingly and half reluctantly, as her job has been effectively reduced from an important 18-hours-a-day occupation, crucial to society's survival, to a marginal three-hours-per-day activity, almost as easily done by someone else.

WOMEN FIGHT TO HOLD ONTO MOTHERHOOD

Every occupational group fights for survival when threatened with technological obsolescence and tries to retain a monopoly over its technical skills. Women—or, rather, mothers (the words are still almost interchangeable)—are no exception: Mothers continue to apply their customary technical skills even when unnecessary or even undesirable. Tender care turns into over-control; attention into excessive scrutiny. In an effort to maintain their traditional 18-hours-a-day, useful, respected job in the face of its reduced tasks, mothers have been developing an obsession with the details of their children's internal lives, trivial social behavior, and interpersonal attitudes. The mothers simply have nothing else to do. They use guilt to bind their children, even when grown, to themselves, for their children are their only occupational tools and source of commitment. To give up their two or three over-manipulated children would mean retirement.

GUILT-RIDDEN CHILDREN SCREAM FOR FREEDOM

Mothers' use of guilt to bind their children has had massive psychological consequences, and happily not all are bad. This relatively new socialization form may help adapt the industrial personality to the post-industrial realities of the future. Guilt has made middle-class children introspective and self-conscious, to a degree never before known in the western world. Psychological manipulation now is so common that adolescents are uniting in their mutual sense of victimization. They identify with and feel responsible for all victims and, in the process of seeking redress of wrongs, they are changing the values of the culture. This is happening at a time when our technological capacities can permit the fulfillment of the responsibilities that are felt toward all economic, social, and psychological victims.

Our young people have been mothered to death: They have been subject to a level of scrutiny and maternal investment and guilt that paralyzes them and makes them crawl the walls and scream for freedom. They long for real internal choice—not choice forced on them by guilt—and they are presenting us with magnificent new possibilities for freedom in the 21st century.

The overinjection of guilt has turned young people against the capitalistic system, which has demanded competition and aggression; their mothers taught them to hate aggression and to feel guilty about expressing it. At the same time, the young people have been turned against the Protestant Ethic with its too crass, too simplistic, and too visible exploitation of external guilt. Among the young people, internal guilt has replaced external guilt; instead of feeling guilty when they have done something defined as evil, they feel guilty when they have only thought of doing something evil or even when they have merely failed to do something good.

This internal guilt continues to bloom and produce even more internal or maternal guilt, now shared by sons and daughters alike, because it is the only form of socialization that is truly familiar to our middle-class young people. *Portnoy's Complaint* was a commercial success because so many people recognized its portrayal of motherhood. What is not always appreciated is that Mother Portnoy produced, by her seductiveness and massive injection of guilt, a Commissioner of Human Rights, a champion of victims.

The larger-than-life quality of the American mother and her method of control—seduction and guilt—have produced a whole generation of men who have overidentified with their mothers and of women who fear being like their mothers. Many of the young women now liberating themselves are committed to avoiding the traps that their own mothers were caught in. Young men, overidentified with their seductive, nurturing mothers, want to release women from the restrictive roles that damage everyone. These men are willing to let women change and to help them so that another generation of children will not be exposed to the seduction and guilt that they experienced in their own childhood. The young men wear their hair long, carry babies on their back, and oppose war. The young women wear pants, defiantly assert their independence and initiative, and spend less time making marriage traps for men.

"MAMA SOCIALIZATION" WILL INCREASE CREATIVITY

Young people tend to see the new outlook in moral terms, but behind the new moralities lie economic necessities. The "mama technique"—seduction, guilt, and the suppression of aggression—is emerging as the technique of the future—the electronic, post-industrial society. The old "papa technique," based on authority, fear, and punishment, is less useful for creative mind tasks, and the rise of computer technology is increasing the value placed on creative thinking, which does not flower in the face of threats. As we shift from the dominance of physical power to the dominance of mental power, fear and punishment become useless. The emphasis on guilt, which prevents the expression of aggression, on seduction rather than fear, and on psychological manipulation and self-consciousness, has prepared the way for the emerging electronic society, which will emphasize mind skills rather than physical skills, knowledge cooperatively produced rather than material goods competitively produced, creative thinking rather than behavioral conformity, and the quality of psychological life rather than the quality of material life. Creative work demands sublimated aggression. Complex organizational involvement (which will be the lot of everyone) and the increase in temporary, voluntary relationships will also demand that aggression be suppressed. We are becoming too dependent on each other to allow the open expression of aggression in organizational life. People can attack each other freely only when they don't need each other desperately. Through their mothers' emphasis on guilt, men and women are both learning to suppress aggression very effectively.

WOMEN WILL SHIFT TO OTHER OCCUPATIONS

In the immediate future, we shall see women shifting the skills already developed and incorporated into their identity system to new occupations akin to the old. Women will put their socialization and seductive skills to work in other frameworks. Already, women are moving in large numbers into the burgeoning service industries which need the very skills in which women have been trained since babyhood. Eventually, women will be the policy-makers of those industries that deal in one way or another with issues of human motivation and internal needs—arts, entertainment, advertising, social services, education, etc.—for these fields all require what has already been defined as women's way of winning: covertly, patiently, by influence rather than power, by bewitchment and provocativeness rather than force and demand. Women will fan out into still-unimagined forms of education, and will work with "dependents" other than small children, such as the adult underprivileged and marginal, the elderly, the mentally ill, and any other categories of people who need, like children, to have their competencies developed.

In perhaps 20 or 30 years, feminine virtues will be diffused through the society, because women—the traditional repositories of these virtues—will have begun to lose their defined occupational role. Men will incorporate characteristics that were previously defined as female virtues, partly because they will want to, out of identification with their mothers, but also because economic conditions will require it. Women will incorporate virtues previously defined as male, due to their industrial involvement and independence. The result will be a greater richness in the human character. We will find independence coupled with yieldingness and compromise, thrust coupled with tenderness, adventure and experiment coupled with stability, decision-making and responsibility coupled with guilt.

Ultimately, when women have a free choice of economic roles and their identities are no longer tied to motherhood and the traditional feminine virtues associated with it, we may be quite surprised to discover that no more women will choose to be mothers than men would choose to be engineers—and that kind of choice is what is needed if we are to solve the population problem.

MEN AND WOMEN WILL CONVERGE OCCUPATIONALLY

Unisex will come into fashion as a consequence of free choice. Nothing will distinguish men and women, socially and occupationally, from each other, since they will merge the features now kept so carefully in cubby-holes.

After the transition is complete, there will be men and women in all fields, but the distribution of the sexes in the occupations will not be completely random. Differences between men and women based on differences in their biological equipment will result in some slight but non-random differences in the percentage of each sex in certain occupations. Biology will be expressed in a new way. Men sexually "penetrate," and throughout history, they have abstracted and extended this perspective and skill into work in the real world. They have always specialized in exploration, thrust, depth, and analysis. Women sexually "incorporate" and they will abstract and extend this skill to work in the future electronic world which will emphasize incorporation and synthesis ("bringing it together") and integration. The sexual incorporativeness of women will be expressed in non-sexual ways, just as the sexual penetrativeness of men will appear in non-sexual ways. The preference for analytic penetration, on the one hand, or integrative incorporation, on the other, will give each sex an edge in different fields.

The rapidly increasing specialization of knowledge and social change will create a demand for coherence and stability. There will thus be a need for increasing numbers of integrative incorporators or incorporative integrators, that is, coordinators of knowledge and meaning. Economically, the rise of computer technology, and the knowledge industries will require an army of "synthesizers," "pattern recognizers," "integrators," and "information shapers." Women will have a very slight natural edge in integrative fields just as men will continue to have a slight edge in exploratory, penetrating fields. The best synthesizers will tend to be women and the best explorers will tend to be men. Penetration will remain critical at the frontiers of knowledge and social change, but the synthesis of knowledge and meaning will become increasingly crucial.

If we are to understand the relationship between technological change and our human future, we must understand that by transforming human lives and expectations, *technology transforms human character.* Technology's deepest impact is on human perceptions and motives, which it shapes through the daily events of our lives. If we want to predict the future, we must understand precisely how technology can alter the way we feel and think. This understanding may come as much from an acute re-examination of our past as in the scenario building of our future.

the rising problem of "single parents"

Emerging as an important factor in American life is a rapidly growing army of "single parents"—the divorced, the widowed, the unwed mothers and bachelor fathers.

Life for many of them is difficult—in some cases bitterly so—as they encounter an avalanche of financial, legal, social and psychological problems.

Yet, since 1965, the number of such families has gone up 31.4 percent, almost triple the growth registered for two-parent families.

Today, single-parent families total 8.1 million, or 14.9 percent of the nation's 54 million families. Single parents are raising about 8.6 million youngsters under 18, or about 13 per cent of the national total.

As a result, Americans are becoming increasingly aware of this growing minority and related questions of federal child-care subsidies, allegedly unfair taxes they must pay, discrimination by credit institutions, and the well-being of single-parent children.

THE DIVORCE FACTOR

As the chart on page 86 shows, most of the growth in single-parent families is developing out of the explosive rise in U. S. divorces.

Whether divorced, widowed or never married, many single parents are finding that they must contend with problems for which most have had little preparation. George B. Williams, executive di-

Reprinted from *U. S. News & World Report,* July 16, 1973.
Copyright 1973 U. S. News & World Report, Inc.

THE SHARP INCREASE IN ONE-PARENT FAMILIES

FAMILIES HEADED BY FATHERS ALONE

	1965	1972	CHANGE
Widowers	443,000	480,000	Up 8%
Divorced, separated males	208,000	365,000	Up 71%
Single males	426,000	410,000	Down 4%

FAMILIES HEADED BY MOTHERS ALONE

	1965	1972	CHANGE
Widows	2,301,000	2,370,000	Up 3%
Divorced, separated females	1,731,000	2,743,000	Up 58%
Single females	397,000	713,000	Up 80%

THUS: Fastest growth in one-parent families has come among divorced or separated mates and unwed mothers.

Source: U. S. Census Bureau.

rector of Parents Without Partners, an international organization based in Washington, D. C., explained:

"The end of a marriage, especially if children are involved, is for most people a traumatic experience.

"Even if problems are anticipated, nobody ever expects them to be so critical. The frequent responses are demoralization and despair."

POORER LIVING

Almost all families who lose a parent are finding their expenses higher and their income lower. As a result, such families are forced to cut down their standard of living.

Often, single parents start off with sizable debts. Example: Louis Pastor, a certified public accountant in New York City who raised a son and a daughter alone, said that his wife's terminal illness—cancer —lasted several years, with medical bills amounting to "at least $10,000."

In his case, a good job and insurance policies covered much of the cost. But most women who raise children by themselves are not as fortunate. Few are employed or even have job skills, and most are initially dependent mainly on whatever financial arrangements have been made for them.

For widows, these may include their husbands' insurance policies, pensions, Social Security benefits, and family savings. Results vary widely, from a comfortable living for some widowed mothers and their children, to a bare-bones existence for others.

UNCERTAINTIES OF ALIMONY

However small the widow's stipend, it is certain income—more certain than alimony and child-support payments for divorcées.

In theory, divorcées can receive alimony for the rest of their lives—or at least until they remarry. In fact, reports indicate most are getting it for only two years or so.

Child-support payments are supposed to continue until the children reach the age of majority, which is being lowered to 18 in many States.

What such payments mean is that many ex-husbands in the U. S. are paying 35 to 40 percent—and sometimes as much as 75 percent—of their incomes in alimony and child support. As a result, 90 percent eventually default on the payments. Ralph Podell, circuit judge of Milwaukee County, Wis., and chairman of the American Bar Association's family-law section, said:

"It's tragic—and there is no real solution to the problem. Most couples are so deeply in debt when they divorce that there's not enough money for one household, let alone two."

Most States allow courts to exact stiff punishments—including jail terms—for those who default on their payments. But wives generally are reluctant to take the matter to court. For example, a Mexican-American divorcée in Houston said she is supposed to receive $100 a month from her former husband. But, she said:

"I had to take him to court once before when he got behind in payments. He still owes me $400, but I've quit fighting it. If I had him put in jail, I wouldn't get anything."

JOBS A NECESSITY

Widows and divorcées who head families usually must lose little time in looking for additional sources of income. The Women's Bureau of the Labor Department reports that 53 percent of female heads of families are in the labor market—either working or looking for jobs. Many enter the job market untrained, and are having to take low-paying jobs—as office workers, sales clerks, or waitresses—though they may have high-school diplomas or college degrees.

In that situation, the median income for families headed by women in 1971 came to $5,114, little more than half of the $9,208 income for single-parent families headed by white men. For families headed by black women, the median income was only $3,645—considerably below the poverty level of $4,137 for a family of four set for that year by the Federal Government.

A major expense that is hitting hardest at single parents is day care for their children, which can cost $1,500 or more annually for each youngster under the age of 6.

Even if they have the money, the parents are running into a shortage of qualified day-care centers. In 1970, when working mothers —with or without husbands—had more than 6 million children under 6 years old, there were licensed day-care centers for only 625,000.

As alternatives, some mothers are arranging with relatives or friends to care for their children while they work. Others hire baby-sitters.

GOVERNMENT AID

Since 1967, hundreds of thousands of low-income working women have received government subsidies for child-care services, with the Federal Government paying 75 percent of the subsidies and the States paying the rest. This enables many children to get care at no charge and others to get it at greatly reduced rates.

Caspar Weinberger, Secretary of Health, Education and Welfare, estimates that in the year that ended June 30 a total of 694,000 children were enrolled in government-subsidized day care.

The Federal Government has put a ceiling on the mushrooming social-services budget, which includes day-care subsidies, and stiffened eligibility requirements. Secretary Weinberger insists that restrictions will not block the growth of subsidized day-care rolls to nearly 1 million in the year ending next June 30.

Many single parents benefiting from the program are claiming that the new rules will inflict real hardship.

For example, Kay Eisenhower, a billing clerk at Highland General Hospital in Oakland, Calif., said that the cost to her of sending her 4-year-old son to a day-care center—if his subsidy is withdrawn—could triple.

To help ease the burden of child care for low- and middle-income women workers, Congress in 1971 liberalized the Income Tax Act. Day-care costs up to $400 a month or $4,800 a year became tax deductible for anybody earning $18,000 a year or less. Above that income, tax deductions for day care are gradually reduced, so that persons making $27,600 or more receive no deductions at all.

MIDDLE-CLASS PINCH

Many single parents are complaining that this new system still works a hardship on middle-class families. Being heard increasingly is the argument that day-care expenses should be considered a legitimate business expense, entirely deductible.

"If some corporate executive decides he needs two secretaries for his office, the whole cost of their salaries is tax deductible," says one irate New York City widow. "Yet, when a woman needs to hire a housekeeper to look after her children, so that she can work, only a portion of the expense—and perhaps none at all—may be deductible."

The low salaries paid most women and the difficulty and expense in locating child care is leading many divorcées and widows to the conclusion that working simply is not worthwhile. Instead, they are turning to the welfare rolls. Of the nation's 2.5 million families receiving aid to families with dependent children, more than 80 percent are headed by women.

Husbandless mothers also are running into trouble in making such "normal" financial arrangements as getting credit cards, buying a house or a car, or even insuring the car—as required by law in many states.

POOR CREDIT RISKS?

Divorcées and widows are often considered poor risks, and some companies automatically refuse to do business with them—except on a cash-only basis. Women sometimes cannot get credit even from companies which extended credit to their husbands.

"When I got the divorce," says Mrs. Diane Meyers, a Houston secretary, "I discovered I didn't have any credit. I didn't have a car and couldn't get a loan to buy one. I even had trouble finding a place to live, because apartment owners feared that a divorced woman could not give proper supervision to the children. Without some money my mother left me when she died, I never would have made it."

Some widows are solving the dilemma by leaving credit accounts in their husbands' names, even though the husband is dead. Here is one reason why: A widow in Washington, D.C., tried to change credit cards from her late husband's name to her own, but was turned down as a poor risk. Much later, to her surprise, one of the credit-card companies increased the amount of credit extended to her husband, apparently unaware he was dead. Says a friend:

"It has become obvious to her that a man who has been dead six years has a higher credit standing than a working widow."

CONGRESS ALERTED

Several bills have been introduced in Congress to correct these ills. One would amend the 1968 Fair Housing Act, making it illegal to refuse a woman a mortgage simply because of her sex. Another would amend the Truth-in-Lending Act to eliminate the same kind of discrimination in consumer lending.

The problems of unwed mothers are even greater than those of widows and divorcées. For them, there is no widow's pension or alimony payment.

An example is Maria, who has a 2-year-old son in San Francisco. She gets by on $190 a month in public-assistance payment and what she can earn part time.

Maria shares a two-bedroom apartment with another unwed mother who has a 2-year-old daughter. The women split room-and-board costs and take turns baby-sitting for each other.

Maria, who has attended college, has had several jobs, but says they were "rotten," adding: "I have no plans to go back to that kind of existence."

Instead, she plans to develop her talents for dancing, jewelry making, writing and organizing benefits. Her son, she says, is to get an "alternative education—not public school—so that he can develop his potential."

DAMAGE TO CHILDREN

Beyond financial worries is an even bigger one for many single parents —the impact on their children of "a broken home."

Child and family experts generally agree that children need the influence of both a mother and a father in their home life. When one of the parents is missing, they say normal development of the young can be deflected.

Some authorities on delinquency report that the rising tide of single-parent families helps account for the doubling in juvenile-court cases from 1960 to 1971, when youngsters 10 through 17 increased by only 30 percent.

Their argument is this: Children from broken homes, boiling with anger and resentment over the loss of a parent—usually a father, thus leaving them without a father's guidance and discipline—can succumb to antisocial behavior such as bullying, truancy, vandalism or worse.

Mrs. Justine Wise Polier, a recently retired family-court judge in New York City, tells this story:

"One boy, whose parents had divorced, kept running away from home—even though it seemed to be a good home. He was never able to explain his reasons, until he finally blurted out: 'I'm looking for my father.' "

Still, Mrs. Polier and other juvenile experts point out that delinquency cannot be blamed solely upon broken homes. Dr. Richard A. Gardner, a child psychiatrist at Columbia University and author of "The Boys and Girls Book About Divorce," warns:

"It is a vast oversimplification to say that a broken home turns a child into a delinquent. Some become delinquent, but many do not."

DELINQUENCY CAUSE

Even more than the lack of a second parent in a home, such experts conclude, it is friction and hostility between two parents that scars children and encourages delinquency. These experts add that much of today's juvenile crime is occurring among the children of quarrelsome but still-married parents.

Developing as a bigger worry than delinquency for many single parents are signs of deep neurosis in their children. These children are caught between fears of losing the remaining parent and the hope of someday regaining the missing father or mother.

One woman in New York City became a widow when her daughter was 5 years old and remarried several years later. She remembers:

"At first my daughter wouldn't let my new husband sit in her father's chair. She couldn't give up the hope that her father would return someday, and she couldn't get used to the idea that she had to share me with this stranger. He reacted very well, though, and treated her as an uncle would, instead of a new father. They get along very well now."

Children's readjustment problems often are made even more difficult when caught in the middle of parental claims.

In 90 percent of all divorce cases, women are granted custody of the children. Increasingly, however, courts are deciding that the father is the more fit parent and granting him custody. Court battles over custody and visiting rights are becoming more common—and are often producing emotional problems for the single parents, their ex-spouses and the children.

Such legal fights, it has been found, tend to heighten strain and —sometimes—unpleasantness between divorced parents and their children, especially on visiting day.

"The problem is that too many divorced couples make the children pawns in their personal wars," said Judge Podell. "Many are selfish and self-centered—more concerned with their own rights and privileges than those of the children."

The result, the child-care experts say, is to trap children in divided loyalties, making it difficult for them to show affection for one parent without feeling they have betrayed the other.

Even without such strains, divorced or widowed parents can find it hard to readjust to the simple fact of being single again. For many, running a household alone becomes quite complicated. A Houston divorcée pointed out:

"I have to work to make a living, and I'm going to school to improve my ability to do so. I try to spend as much time with my children as possible. But there's not much time left for me, and I need that."

EMOTIONAL HAZARDS

Family counselors, furthermore, note that loneliness, caused by the absence of another adult in the household, is depriving many single parents of the companionship and counsel they need.

"Couples can talk over their problems and decide what to do," said Dr. Hanna Kapit, a psychoanalyst at New York City's Post Graduate Center for Psychotherapy. "Most married women, during their housework each day, look forward to their husband's coming home, so they can have a relaxed, adult conversation. Single parents don't have that."

Many find that they no longer fit in with their married friends—and learn that it is difficult to meet eligible members of the opposite sex. For this reason, many single parents are joining "singles" groups or going to "singles" night clubs, which are frequented by people interested in making new friends.

For some, this is working out. A widower in New York City, for example, found that the experience helped end the long period of depression following his wife's death.

Others find singles groups depressing—in some cases a haven for neurotics and those in search of sex partners. A San Francisco widow said:

"I was coaxed to go to a singles-group affair one time. There was supposed to be an opportunity for conversation, but it was loud music, dim lighting and too many sad, lonely people. I didn't stay long."

SOCIAL OUTLETS

Still, single parents, especially widows and divorcées have a need for recreation, Dr. Kapit said. She added:

"Being a good mother can be very satisfying—but not exclusive of everything else. Every woman has a brain that needs to be stimulated. She needs a social outlet. And most human beings need close contact with a friend of the opposite sex."

To solve their common problems, and to provide social outlets, single parents are beginning to band together in organizations around the country.

Parents Without Partners—the largest and oldest of these—claims 85,000 members in 700 chapters around the country. It offers counseling, seminars and social activities for members and children.

Many women, who disapprove of what they call "mate chasing" activities of Parents Without Partners, have formed a new organization called Momma, headquartered in the Los Angeles area, which spurns such activities.

Most single parents eventually remarry. And during the single period, most manage to make it through.

SUCCESS STORIES

Examples everywhere tell of single parents running households by themselves, raising responsible children and even enjoying their new life styles. Says a home economist in Los Angeles, herself a widow:

"I can name seven broken families that I know, all with great kids, with no serious worries. I think the reason is that there is a closer relationship between parent and child than normally. They are working closely together, and they are feeling needed.

"The children may mature faster, but at the same time, they are learning to take responsibility for themselves, and they will be better prepared for life and marriage."

Chapter 11

parenthood training or mandatory birth control: take your choice

Roger W. McIntire

Few parents like to be told how to raise their children, and even fewer will like the idea of someone telling them whether they can even have children in the first place. But that's exactly what I'm proposing—the licensing of parenthood. Of course, civil libertarians and other liberals will claim this would infringe the parents' rights to freedom of choice and equal opportunity. But what about the rights of children? Surely the parents' competence will influence their children's freedom and opportunity. Today, any couple has the right to try parenting, regardless of how incompetent they might be. No one seems to worry about the unfortunate subjects of their experimenting.

The idea of licensing parenthood is hardly new. But until recently, our ignorance of environmental effects, our ignorance of contraception, and our selfish bias against the rights of children have inhibited public discussion of the topic. In recent years, however, psychologists have taught us just how crucial the effect of the home environment can be, and current research on contraception appears promising.

CONTRACEPTION BY CAPSULE

Successful control of parenthood will require a contraceptive that remains in effect until it is removed or counteracted by the administration of a second drug. Sheldon Segal, director of Rockefeller University's Biomedical Division of the Population Council has developed (with others) a contraceptive capsule implant and has clinically tested it. Inserted under a woman's skin by hypodermic needle, the capsule leaks a steady supply of progestin, which prevents pregnancy. A three-year capsule is now being perfected. A doctor could terminate the contraceptive effect early merely by removing the capsule.

Several scientists are currently conducting research on a contraceptive by which a man's sperm could be rendered inoperative. Leslie A. and Charles F. Westoff, authors of *From Now to Zero: Fertility, Contraception and Abortion in America,* describe a procedure that strengthens the fluids that surround the sperm cells and prohibit fertilization. (Ordinarily, female enzymes in the uterus destroy this protection so that the sperm may fertilize.) Philip Rumke, head of the Department of Immunology at the Netherlands Cancer Institute, and Roberto Mancini, professor of Histology at the Buenos Aires Medical School have both been experimenting with contraceptive vaccines that would inactivate male sperm.

THE CHILD VICTIM

Clearly, we will soon have the technology necessary to carry out a parenthood licensing program, and history tells us that whenever we develop a technology, we inevitably use it. We should now be concerned with developing the criteria for good parenthood. In some extreme cases we already have legal and social definitions. We obviously consider child abuse wrong, and look upon those who physically mistreat their children as bad parents. In some states the courts remove children from the custody of parents convicted of child abuse.

In a recent review of studies of child-abusing parents, John J. Spinetta and David Rigler concluded that such people are generally ignorant of proper child-rearing practices. They also noted that many child-abusing parents had been victims of abuse and neglect in their own youth. Thus our lack of control over who can be parents magnifies the problem with each generation.

In the case of child abusing parents, the state attempts to prevent the most obvious physical mistreatment of children. At this extreme, our culture does demand that parents prove their ability to provide for the physical well-being of their children. But our culture makes almost no demands when it comes to the children's psychological well-being and development. Any fool can now raise a child any way he or she pleases, and it's none of our business. The child becomes the unprotected victim of whoever gives birth to him.

Ironically, the only institutions that do attempt to screen potential parents are the adoption agencies, although their screening can hardly be called scientific. Curiously enough, those who oppose a parent-licensing law usually do not oppose the discriminating policies practiced by the adoption agencies. It seems that our society cares more about the selection of a child's second set of parents than it does about his original parents. In other words, our culture insists on insuring a certain quality of parenthood for adopted children, but if you want to have one of your own, feel free.

Screening and selecting potential parents by no means guarantees that they will in fact be good parents. Yet today we have almost no means of insuring proper child-rearing methods. The indiscriminate "right to parent" enables everyone, however ill-equipped, to practice any parental behavior they please. Often their behavior would be illegal if applied to any group other than children. But because of our prejudice against the rights of children, we protect them only when the most savage and brutal parental behavior can be proved in court. Consider the following example:

SUPERMARKET SCENARIO

A mother and daughter enter a supermarket. An accident occurs when the daughter pulls the wrong orange from the pile and 37 oranges are given their freedom. The mother grabs the daughter, shakes her vigorously, and slaps her. What is your reaction? Do you ignore the incident? Do you consider it a family squabble and none of your business? Or do you go over and advise the mother not to hit her child? If the mother rejects your advice, do you physically restrain her? If she persists, do you call the police? Think about your answers for a moment.

Now let me change one detail. *The girl was not that mother's daughter.* Do you feel different? Would you act differently? Why? Do "real" parents have the right to abuse their children because they "own" them? Now let me change another detail. Suppose the daughter was 25 years old, and yelled, "Help me! Help me!" Calling the police sounded silly when I first suggested it. How does it sound with a mere change in the age of the victim?

Now let's go back to the original scene where we were dealing with a small child. Were you about to advise the mother or insist? Were you going to say she shouldn't or couldn't? It depends on whose rights you're going to consider. If you think about the mother's right to mother as she sees fit, then you advise; but if you think about the child's right as a human being to be protected from the physical assault of this woman, then you insist. The whole issue is obviously tangled in a web of beliefs about individual rights, parental rights, and children's rights. We tend to think children deserve what they get, or at least must suffer it. Assault and battery, verbal abuse, and even forced imprisonment become legal if the victims are children.

When I think about the issue of children's rights, and the current development of new contraceptives, I see a change coming in this country. I'm tempted to make the following prediction in the form of a science-fiction story:

MOTHERHOOD IN THE 1980s

"Lock" was developed as a kind of semipermanent contraceptive in 1975. One dose of Lock and a woman became incapable of ovulation until the antidote "Unlock" was administered. As with most contraceptives, Lock required a prescription, with sales limited by the usual criteria of age and marital status.

Gradually, however, a subtle but significant distinction became apparent. Other contraceptives merely allowed a woman to protect herself against pregnancy at her own discretion. Once Lock was administered, however, the prescription for Unlock required an active decision to allow the *possibility* of pregnancy.

By 1978, the two drugs were being prescribed simultaneously, leaving the Unlock decision in the hands of the potential mother. Of course, problems arose. Mothers smuggled Lock to their daughters and the daughters later asked for Unlock. Women misplaced the Unlock and had to ask for more. Faced with the threat of a black market, the state set up a network of special dispensaries for the contraceptive and its antidote. When the first dispensaries opened in 1979, they dispensed Lock rather freely, since they could always regulate the use of Unlock. But it soon became apparent that special local committees would be necessary to screen applicants for Unlock. "After all," the dispensary officials asked themselves, "how would you like to be responsible for this person becoming a parent?"

Protect Our Children

That same year, 1979, brought the school-population riots. Overcrowding had forced state education officials to take some action. Thanks to more efficient educational techniques, they were able to consider reducing the number of years of required schooling. This, however, would have thrown millions of teen-agers out onto the already overcrowded job market, which would make the unions unhappy. Thus, rather than shortening the entire educational process, the officials decided to shorten the school day into two half-day shifts. That led to the trouble.

Until then, people had assumed that schools existed primarily for the purpose of education. But the decision to shorten the school day exposed the dependence of the nation's parents on the school as the great baby sitter of their offspring. Having won the long struggle for daycare centers, and freedom from diapers and bottles, mothers were horrified at the prospect of a few more hours of responsibility every day until their children reached 18 or 21. They took to the streets [cf. Binstock, p. 78].

In Richmond, Virginia, a neighborhood protest over the shortened school day turned into a riot. One of the demonstrators picked up a traffic sign near the school that cautioned drivers to "Protect Our Children," and found herself leading the march toward city hall. Within a week that sign became the national slogan for the protesters, as well as for the Lock movement. It came to mean not only protecting our children from overcrowding and lack of supervision, but also protecting them from pregnancy.

Because of the school-population riots, distribution of Lock took on the characteristics of an immunization program under the threat of an epidemic. With immunization completed, the state could control the birth rate like a water faucet by the distribution of Unlock. However this did not solve the problem of deciding who should bear the nation's children.

Congress Takes Over

To settle the issue, Congress appointed a special blue-ribbon commission of psychologists, psychiatrists, educators, and clergymen to come up with acceptable criteria for parenthood, and a plan for a licensing program. The commission issued its report in 1984. Based upon its recommendations, Congress set up a Federal regulatory agency to administer a national parenthood-licensing program similar to driver-training and licensing procedures.

The agency now issues study guides for the courses, and sets the required standards of child-rearing knowledge. Of course, the standards vary for parents, teachers, and child-care professionals, depending upon the degree of responsibility involved. The courses and exams are conducted by local community colleges, under the supervision of the Federal agency. Only upon passing the exams can prospective parents receive a prescription for Unlock.

Distribution of Lock and Unlock is now strictly regulated by the Federal agency's local commissions. Since the records of distribution are stored in Federal computer banks, identification of illegitimate pregnancies (those made possible by the unauthorized use of Unlock) has become a simple matter. Parents convicted of this crime are fined, and required to begin an intensive parenthood-training program immediately. If they do not qualify by the time their child is born, the child goes to a community child-care program until they do.

Drawing the Battle Lines

As might be expected, the parent-licensing program has come under attack from those who complain about the loss of their freedom to create and raise children according to their own choice and beliefs. To such critics, the protect-our-children or Lock faction argues: "It's absurd to require education and a license to drive a car, but allow anybody to raise our most precious possession or to add to the burden of this possession without demonstrating an ability to parent."

"But the creation of life is in the hands of God" say the freedom-and-right-to-parent-faction (referred to by their opposition as the "far-right-people").

"Nonsense," say the Lock people. "Control over life creation was acquired with the first contraceptive. The question is whether we use it with intelligence or not."

"But that question is for each potential parent to answer as an individual" say the far-right people.

The Lock people answer: "those parents ask the selfish question of whether they want a child or not. We want to know if the child will be adequately cared for—by them and by the culture."

The far right respond, "God gave us bodies and all their functions. We have a right to the use of those functions. Unlock should be there for the asking. Why should the Government have a say in whether I have a child?"

"Because the last century has shown that the Government will be saddled with most of the burden of raising your child," say the Lock people. "The schools, the medical programs, the youth programs, the crime-prevention programs, the colleges, the park and planning commissions—they will be burdened with your child. That's why the Government should have a say. The extent of the Government's burden depends on your ability to raise your child. If you screw it up, the society *and* Government will suffer. That's why they should screen potential parents."

From the right again: "The decision of my spouse and myself is sacred. It's none of their damn business."

But the Locks argue: "If you raised your child in the wilderness and the child's malfunctions punished no one but yourselves, it would be none of their damn business. But if your child is to live with us, be educated by us, suffered by us, add to the crowd of us, we should have a say."

FACE OF THE FUTURE

I can understand how some people might find this story either far-fetched or frightening, but I don't think any prediction in it is too far in the future. Carl Djerassi suggested the possibility of a semi-permanent contraceptive such as "Lock" and "Unlock" (although he didn't use those brand names) as early as 1969, in an article in *Science*. And as I described earlier, other scientists are currently making significant strides in contraceptive research.

Throughout history, as knowledge has eroded away superstition about conception and birth, humans have taken increasing control over the birth of their offspring. Religious practices, arranged marriages, mechanical and biochemical contraception have all played a role in this regulation of procreation. Until now, however, such regulation has dealt only with the presence or absence of children, leaving their development to cultural superstitions. Anyone with normal biology may still produce another child, and, within the broadest limits, treat it any way he or she chooses.

We have taken a long time in coming to grips with this problem because our society as a whole has had no demonstrably better ideas about child-rearing than any individual parent. And until now, people couldn't be stopped from having children because we haven't had the technology that would enable us to control individual fertility.

HOW TO REAR A CHILD

The times are changing. With the population problem now upon us, we can no longer afford the luxury of allowing any two fools to add to our numbers whenever they please. We do have, or soon will have, the technology to control individual procreation. And, most important, psychology and related sciences have by now established some child-rearing principles that should be part of every parent's knowledge. An objective study of these principles need not involve the prying, subjective investigation now used by adoption agencies. It would merely insure that potential parents would be familiar with the principles of sound child-rearing. Examinations and practical demonstrations would test their knowledge. Without having state agents check every home (and of course, we would never accept such "Big Brother" tactics) there could be no way to enforce the use of that knowledge. But insistence on the knowledge would itself save a great deal of suffering by the children.

The following list suggests a few of the topics with which every parent should be familiar:

1 Principles of sound nutrition and diet.

2 Changes in nutritional requirements with age.

3 Principles of general hygiene and health.

4 Principles of behavioral development: normal range of ages at which behavioral capabilities might be expected, etc.

5 Principles of learning and language acquisition.

6 Principles of immediacy and consistency that govern parents' reactions to children's behavior.

7 Principles of modeling and imitation: how children learn from and copy their parents' behavior.

8 Principles of reinforcement: how parent and peer reactions reward a child's behavior, and which rewards should be used.

9 Principles of punishment: how parents' reactions can be used to punish or discourage bad behavior.

10 Response-cost concept: how to "raise the cost" or create unpleasant consequences in order to make undesirable behavior more "expensive" or difficult.

11 Extinction procedures and adjunctive behavior: if rewards for good behavior cease, children may "act up" just to fill the time.

12 Stimulus-control generalization: children may act up in some situations, and not in others, because of different payoffs. For example, Mommy may give the child candy to stop a tantrum, whereas Daddy may ignore it or strike the child.

Most of us have some familiarity with the principles at the beginning of this list, but many parents have little knowledge of the other topics. Some psychologists would obviously find my list biased toward behavior modification, but their revisions or additions to the list only strengthen my argument that our science has a great deal to teach that would be relevant to a parenthood-licensing program.

MISPLACED PRIORITIES

Of course the word licensing suggests that the impersonal hand of Government may control individual lives, and that more civil servants will be paid to meddle in our personal affairs. But consider for a moment that for our safety and well-being we already license pilots, salesmen, scuba divers, plumbers, electricians, teachers, veterinarians, cab drivers, soil testers and television repairmen. To protect pedestrians, we accept restrictions on the speed with which we drive our cars. Why, then, do we encounter such commotion, chest thumping, and cries of oppression when we try to protect the well-being of children by controlling the most crucial determiner of that well-being, the competence of their parents? Are our TV sets and toilets more important to us than our children? Can you image the public outcry that would occur if adoption agencies offered their children on a first-come-first-served basis, with no screening process for applicants? Imagine some drunk stumbling up and saying, "I'll take that cute little blond-haired girl over there."

We require appropriate education for most trades and professions, yet stop short at parenthood because it would be an infringement on the individual freedom of the parent. The foolishness of this position will become increasingly apparent the more confident we become in our knowledge about child rearing.

The first step toward a parenthood law will probably occur when child-abuse offenders will be asked or required to take "Lock" as an alternative to, or in addition to, being tried in court. Or the courts may also offer the child abuser the alternative of a remedial training program such as the traffic courts now use. The next step may be the broadening of the term "child abuse" to include ignorant mistreatment of a psychological nature. Some communities may add educational programs to marriage-license requirements, while others may add parenthood training to existing courses in baby care.

When the Government gets around to setting criteria for proper child rearing, these must be based upon a very specific set of principles of nutrition, hygiene, and behavior control. They cannot be based on bias and hearsay. Some of the criteria now used by adoption agencies, such as references from neighbors and friends, cannot be considered objective. We don't interview your neighbors when you apply for a driver's license, and it shouldn't be done for a parent's license either. But just as a citizen must now demonstrate knowledge and competence to drive a car, so ought he to demonstrate his ability to parent as well. Proof of exposure to education is not enough. We are not satisfied merely with driver-training courses, but demand a driver's test as well. We should require the same standards of parents.

We can hope that as progress occurs in the technology of contraception and the knowledge of child-rearing principles, the currently sacred "right to parent" will be re-evaluated by our society. Perhaps we can construct a society that will also consider the rights that children have to a humane and beneficial upbringing.

psychological reverberations

Change the roles, functions and relative positions of men and women in any society, and you immediately coerce every individual in that society to adapt emotionally and psychologically to the new roles, functions, and positions. This adaptation is often very painful because it forces us to reevaluate and often change our most personal values and attitudes about the relationships of men and women. Such adaptations have occurred in the past, but then they were either minor changes or spread out over decades and centuries. Today's economic and sexual liberation of humans is not minor; nor is it taking centuries to accomplish. Witness, as just one bit of evidence, the shift in American values regarding premarital sex: in 1969, fully sixty-eight percent of the American population viewed premarital sex as immoral; in 1973, that negative view had dropped twenty points to a minority of forty-eight percent condemning premarital sex. Only twenty-nine percent of those under thirty viewed premarital sex as wrong.

Women feel this revolution most directly, for they are the prime personae in this drama, both as catalyzers and as subjects. Their responses range from the psychology of consciousness-raising sessions, to specific political actions to provide day-care centers, equal pay, no-fault divorce, the economic recognition of the housewife, the elimination of sexist children's books, and the lobbying of "the sisterhood." But men also agonize and grow with this revolution. In some ways the adaptation is far more painful to men than it is for women.

The four essays in this section deal with the psychological aspects of changing male/female relations. Sidney Callahan offers a feminine view of the sexually liberated woman. Dotson Rader talks of the feminization of the American male, and three psychiatrists look at the "new" impotence of the American male. Finally, Elaine Louie reports on the psychological adaptation of a transexual who spent over twenty years as a male and then underwent surgery to become a female and marry.

In typical Hot-Sex chauvinism, the American male looks forward to the liberation of women with as much ambivalence as he once faced the preliberated Victorian lady. Before the sexual revolution, a nice woman was total mother, nurturer, and domestic support system for her husband. But, in the Victorian mystique, she was also sexually innocent and passive. The Freudian and contraceptive revolutions changed this mystique, replacing it with an equally ambivalent image, as Sidney Callahan points out. The marvel of the "super Bunny," ready to satisfy every male fantasy, is matched by the threat of the castrating "super Bitch" with her insatiable sexual capacity, and the "ominous Butch" liberated by her mature clitoral orgasm from any need for the male.

Sidney Callahan cuts to the quick of the sexually liberated woman, highlighting several Cool-Sex values and attitudes mentioned in earlier essays in this anthology. Sexual liberation means a new sense of discrimination and responsibility, a freedom from mystiques and fantasies imposed by a patriarchal society. "As a self-initiating adult, a liberated woman will not be programmed. . . . No one can automatically tell what free women will do beforehand." Thus, Callahan's comments are very relevant to those expressed in later essays by Ginsberg on "The New Impotence" and by Heilbrun on our androgynous future. Unlike our passing Hot-Sex values, the spontaneous, unprogrammed sexual relations we aim for treasure commitment and responsibility, equality and friendship. As such, sexual liberation will require some radical changes in the traditional male life-style, and in our traditional Hot-Sex male psychology.

A 1970 *Psychology Today* poll reported that slightly over one-third of its male readers "have had difficulty achieving erection." Ann Welbourne at the New York Community Sex Information telephone hotline admits, "It's a flood. You get the feeling that every man in the city is impotent or suffers from premature ejaculation." Four of the five sexologists in a 1971 *Medical Aspects of Human Sexuality* round table discussion agreed that impotence is most definitely increasing.

An informal 1972 report from Harvard University confessed that it was "one of the driest years in history," with the Ivy Leaguers turning to masturbation and/or the town prostitutes. Our informal observations and reports on male-female behavior on college campuses around the country only tend to confirm the image of the psychologically castrated male threatened by the performance anxieties of a Hot-Sex machismo and the inexhaustible sexual appetites of liberated women. Some reports we have received place the rate as high as three out of five males suffering from more than just the occasional and normal inability to have an erection and normal intercourse.

Obviously, from all the evidence, more young men and women are engaging in sexual intercourse today. We can thus expect the frequency of normal natural impotence to also increase. With the new freedom of discussion, we can also expect to be more conscious and open to discussion of male impotence. Hence, the controversial point in the evidence cited above is the disputed question whether today's impotence indicates an expected or an unnatural increase. And if it is an unnatural and serious increase in frequency, can we trace its etiology to the male's psychological and emotional response to the liberated, sexually aggressive female. "This is not a question of women's lib," insists Dr. Ginsberg and his colleagues in the article that follows, "but rather the (result of the) way a man perceives it, that social pressures were perceived by the man as his having to *perform* some demand that he was not ready to satisfy."

Our impression is that we are in fact observing a new form of psychological impotence resulting from the male's inability to cope with the unrealistic but very real hot-sex expectation that he must respond to every invitation with an erection crowned by orgasm and a perfect performance. The young male, whose ego and masculine identity is still not secure, is naturally more affected by this anxiety than the mature male. It is natural that young men, in self-defense, turn to the safety of male "wolf packs" adapted from preadolescent days, and to simple physical relief through masturbation and prostitutes—here he knows the rules of the game.

In this valuable perspective, Ginsberg, Frosch, and Shapiro report on "The New Impotence." Based on their clinical experience, their examples and case histories are not representative of the most common or average experience of the "new" impotence. Their case histories represent the clinical extreme of this syndrome, not its typical form which men suffer with embarrassment but without seeking professional help. Nevertheless, Drs. Ginsberg, Frosch, and Shapiro have helped call our attention to an important psychological repercussion of the sexual revolution.

Biologically and psychologically, the female is hardly the weaker of the two sexes. Exactly the opposite: the male comes out on the short end of any measurement. But the image is there, and with it, the expectation and pressure to perform. Dotson Rader, a vocal spokesman for the New Left, issues a loud call for revolution in our coeducational school system. That system, he argues, is the source of unconscionable and inhumane pressures on the American male which in effect castrate and feminize him, if they do not first kill him.

In our opening review of the many technological and medical advances which have helped create new meanings and images for our understanding of human sexuality and the future of sexual relationships, we mentioned the transexual Paula Grossman (cf. p. 6). No single technology highlights the new meanings and images more strikingly than this development. A human being is born, identified as male or female, and raised and accepted by all in his or her society as such. Then, after some mysterious medical treatment, this individual announces his or her "sex assignment" to the opposite gender. He is now she, or she is now he. If, like Paula Grossman, the original he or she was married and a parent, the situation becomes even more confusing. The validity of all our traditional terms for male, female, marriage, and parenthood is riddled with perplexing questions.

In late 1973, a district judge in Carson City, Nevada, ruled in a child custody case that illustrates this new image very clearly. In 1953, Gay Christensen married a Carson City dentist, Dr. Duane Christian. After four children, the couple divorced, and the mother was granted custody of the children in 1964. In 1970, Gay underwent a transexual operation, and two years later, as Mark A. Randall, remarried. The children's original father learned of the situation and sought to gain custody of his children. The judge spoke with the four girls, ranging in age from eleven to seventeen, and found that their mother "had assumed the father image with them." The girls, according to the judge, "profess great affection for their pseudo father and a great disaffection, bordering upon hate, for their natural father, Duane Christian." Calling the case a "most bizarre and most unusual set of circumstances," and admitting that "it strikes at my personal beliefs and opinions which I have held for many years," the judge rendered his decision: "I am convinced Mark Randall is the better parent for these girls."

Elaine Louie explores the realities of transexual operations today, and touches on some of the psychological adjustments this development brings to the future of sexual relations.

Chapter 12

the future of the sexually liberated woman

Sidney Callahan

What will liberated women do? When we hear that question asked, the real question beneath the question is usually sexual. What will sexually liberated women do?

Liberation, of course, is a tricky concept, and sexual liberation is even more ambiguous. When men bring up women's liberation, all sorts of fantasies tend to spring full grown from the male brow. Male fantasies of female sexual liberation usually come in three unappetizing varieties.

1. First to appear is that perennial male dream, the super Bunny, the playmate of the millennium. This liberated woman is totally acquiescent sexually. Liberation and the perpetual "Yes" of Molly Bloom are equated. Sexual liberation means sexual readiness to participate in every man's sexual needs, desires or whims. Gone are the traditionally troublesome problems of female discrimination and demands.

In the fantasy male underworld, women resist sexually only because they are neurotic and hung-up on sex. If women were no longer inhibited sexually then, of course, they would never refuse. "Let me help you get over your sexual hangups," said the wolf to little Red Riding Hood. "Nice girls and liberated women are no longer virgins, you know. Chastity went out with the horse and carriage and surely any woman can."

In this script the sexually liberated woman will not only leave frigidity behind but she will no longer make demands or seek security in exchange for her sexual favors. In the male fantasy of the newly sexually liberated woman, all claims on him for marriage or support are waived. Liberated women will not want to be tied down to square monogamy or family life. Super Bunnies and perennial playmates don't get men involved in sordid security arrangements. As Hugh Hefner so eloquently pleads the case, "Why do love and commitment have to be confused with sex?" Needless to say, the sexually liberated woman will also take care of contraception and quietly get her own abortions in case of slip-ups. (More young males favor abortion on demand than any other segment of the population.)

2. The second male fantasy of the sexually liberated woman is more disturbing. This version of a sexually liberated woman is the super-Bitch incarnate. She is super-sexual but in a castrating way. She eats men; or else she uses them and leaves them crushed and impotent. This fantasy woman is really a female male of the most exploitative sort. She's the spider to the helpless male fly. Perhaps this fantasy arises from the mother in every man's past who would be truly terrible, if she had sexual power along with every other capacity for control.

In any event, the Bitch image of the sexually liberated woman has women embodying the worst of male aggressive behavior. She competes more fiercely and destroys more thoroughly. Since Masters and Johnson have also shown in their sexual studies that female sexuality is more intense and more inexhaustible than the male's, sexual fear stalks the Bitch mystique. Men who resist and fear women's liberation often have sexual insecurities floating around in their psyches.

3. The third ominous male fantasy of sexually liberated women is that of the Lesbian or Butch. Men fantasize women who may liberate themselves out of heterosexuality altogether. Who needs it? Even a stalwart sexual hero like Norman Mailer once allowed as how he could never equal Lesbian lovemaking. Now really. What a sad commentary on masculine self-confidence. The magazine science fiction stories that appear of parthenogenesis eliminating men from the human race (mostly written by men) are tell-tale signs of insecurity.

The ominous Butch fantasy is the obverse of the Bunny mystique. From the eternal "Yes" to the perpetual "No," an ultimate sexual refusal is feared from women's liberation. So men commonly dismiss the whole movement with taunts of "Butch" and "Bitch." When women are no longer daunted by such insults and accusations, then another weapon of social control becomes obsolete.

A characteristic of real liberation now becomes apparent. A liberated person is first of all liberated from other people's fantasies. A sexually liberated woman is no longer caught up in male fantasies of Woman. She can leave behind stereotypes of bunny, bitch, butch, along with preliberation mystiques of the total mother, nurturer and domestic. When women stop being other-directed by male expectations and fantasies, they are beginning to be liberated.

Unfortunately, as in adolescent rebellion, a woman's rebellion may often still be controlled by the strength of what she's reacting against. The young person who hates his parents is still under their domination. If he does things which he knows they will hate, he is not liberated from childhood. So in a reactionary phase, many women get angry with men and rebel violently against traditional femininity. That only proves their psychic bondage to the past and they are deplorably predictable.

Every two-year-old child will say "no" to everything in order to assert autonomy. That "no" is again predictable in adolescent revolt. But the freedom of adulthood is marked by the unpredictable yes or no. So the truly liberated woman will be truly unpredictable. She will neither conform to past conventions nor present fantasies imposed from without. As a self-initiating adult, a liberated woman will not be programmed. That's what freedom means. You act and react according to your unique individuality in each unique situation, modified by aspiration and appropriateness. No one can automatically tell what free women will do beforehand.

Men who dearly long for women to be predictable will be disappointed. Women will grow out of the generic class category and be as fully individualized as men. Can you imagine Freud asking "What do men want?" He and all the others who lump women together to study them, define them, analyze them and so on, will have to unlump them and give up predictions. Only the conditioned animal salivates at the sound of the buzzer. Women just aren't going to live their lives responding to men or society's stereotypes. But a few good guesses into the future are in order.

More women may be among the "self-actualized persons" studied by Maslow long ago. The men and women in the group were more alike (unisexual?) than not, but they were very much themselves in not worrying over their uniqueness. People who have got it all together, as the saying goes, don't worry much about roles and sexual identity. They are satisfied in their work, love and play. They don't even worry about sex.

I think the sexually liberated woman displays the characteristics of Erikson's mature genitality, or of his sexual utopia. Mature genitality is only what you might expect from common sense and careful observation of people we all know. Utopian sex is not separated from love, affection, work, play or personal commitment. The whole relationship between persons is strong enough so that the irrational ecstatic frenzy (and yes fantasy) of sex can be enjoyed securely. Mutual trust and maturity enhances pleasure and playfulness.

Women who have not been equal have had a hard time being mutual. Not trusting themselves, it was hard to trust a man (or vice versa). When the suppression of aggression was thought to be feminine, the suppression of female sexual fulfillment was inevitable. Aggression is as much a part of sexual fulfillment as tenderness. The sexual surrender bit sold to women was mostly a way to guarantee undemand-ing acquiescence. If there is any surrender involved, it is a surrender to one's own aggressive desires for sexual fulfillment.

Women who were the keepers of morality and the guardians of the family are still conditioned to be sexually careful. (Maybe it's even biological.) Well and good, as long as it is appropriate. But sexual in-hibition can be overdone personally and culturally; and nice women in the west have overdone it. Now that control of fertility has relieved women from choosing between sexual fulfillment and the good of their children, they must unlearn inappropriate inhibition.

Most women have been sexually constricted, just as the Chinese bound feminine feet and hobbled their women. Now that new oppor-tunities for social and intellectual self-fulfillment and self-confidence are open to women, so, too, their sexuality will flourish. Mature women have long been more sexually attuned than younger women and it is interesting to wonder whether this is because of physiology or the in-creased self-confidence of older women. Of course, the fact that many young women are so fatigued during their childbearing years may have something to do with it. At any rate, a new appreciation of the mature post-maternal, post-menopausal woman may be finally coming to America, heretofore the land of "The Girl."

Part of the new acceptance of women as women will be a new acceptance of maternity. When women are no longer forced into child-bearing or valued only for their procreative powers, they themselves can fully affirm maternity. The *zeitgeist* on these matters can be ap-praised from watching maternity fashions, and today's maternity clothes are reaching new heights of beauty. Another more important sign is whether women are demanding childcare provisions so they can combine work and motherhood.

When women are femininely self-confident they are not willing to sacrifice either maternity or the fulfillment of other talents. Why should they be penalized for having babies? Or be segregated from the mainstream, or the world of work? Most women will no longer pretend that they are men in order to have careers. Let the institutions adjust to women and children, not force women and children to adjust to male power structures. Liberated women will make more than just sexual demands.

The same feelings of feminine self-confidence, self-worth and strength make women good at mothering and good at work. Women who are good at one, are usually good at the other. It has been a sense-less system that has denied mothers access to the professions and politics. As, among other things, more unmarried women choose to keep their babies, it is imperative that cooperative childrearing arrangements and childcare support be given to women. Liberated women have a right to demand that the whole society help support the new generation, instead of making a child's welfare depend on whether its mother has a man to help her economically. Women who are divorced or deserted also face this crucial issue and will be making more demands. Liberated women are not willing to be allowed into the establishment only if they leave their inconvenient children behind.

Just as women with children will refuse to be penalized, so single women will refuse to be harried because they do not have sexual partners. Since liberated women are no longer judged solely by the men in their life, single women can be self-fulfilled. Work, social life and many other relationships need not be patterned upon Noah's strictures of going into the Ark two by two. A flood is not threatening the end of all human reproduction, but rather the opposite case. Single women and celibates are not socially irresponsible, destined to immaturity, or embarked on an anguished search for their other half.

Liberated married women certainly do not see themselves as half-persons. A couple complement each other, and they cooperate, but their unity is not that of opposites. Each couple is not trying to be a complete isolated universe with each sex taking half the human characteristics and half the human roles. Women (and men) can surely be liberated into flexible roles and divisions of labor. Neither maintenance nor leisure should be the prerogative of one sex. Everyone in a family or household should do what they can to sustain it, and share equally in the rewards.

If women are liberated out of being the sole domestic, men are liberated from being the sole bearer of the mortgage. As for the children of liberated women, it's good for them to lose their maternal slave and chauffeur. The friendship, partnerhood and alliance of liberated parents give an important model to their children. Power can be exercised in cooperation, and that's an important early lesson to learn. Nobody's childhood should be littered with victims. Neither one's mother nor one's father should have done in the other for healthy heterosexuality.

Women who liberate themselves now can help their husbands and children as well. It's especially important that the male child be prevented from an adulthood of distorted fantasies about liberated women. The first woman he knows has a lot to do with his future expectations. And, of course, this is even more true for daughters. If women's sexual and social liberation seems too much of a struggle at times, the thought of our daughters should spur us on. The further we get this time around, the better for them. I fervently hope that an article such as this will seem quaint to the next generation of women. No analysis is needed when you are living your liberation.

Chapter 13

the new impotence

George L. Ginsberg, MD;

William A. Frosch, MD;

and Theodore Shapiro, MD

Advocates of social change argue that when harmful repressions are lifted a more successful adaptation will ensue with improvement of the quality of our lives. We report on one aspect of our changing culture: the effect of increased sexual freedom of women on their male partners. Clinical observations are cited which suggest that this cultural shift is resulting in an increase in complaints of impotence among younger men. Several case histories are presented and we discuss reasons for this additional source of impotence. Rather than more successful adaptation, we suggest that social change may have significant effect on the form of individual psychopathological disturbance. Cultural habits not only rest on repression and inhibition but also support a delicate equilibrium. When this equilibrium is disturbed its dynamic effect may result in the appearance of new maladaptations.

Rapid changes in social mores may be reflected in changes in psychiatric symptomatology. It is our common experience that: (1) young men now appear more frequently with impotence, and (2) young women more frequently complain of initial impotence in their young lovers. We suggest that this may be related to changed social attitudes toward premarital sexuality, particularly among women.

The "average expectable sexual behavior" of the adult woman in certain segments of middle class American society has changed. Although perhaps never real, the generally accepted and religiously prescribed standard of wedding night virginity prevailed well into the 20th century. An acceptable myth separated women into good and bad, with respect to their premarital sexual behavior. Under such conditions many a woman viewed intercourse as something inflicted upon her by her mate and her responsibility consisted of not denying him

"The New Impotence" by George L. Ginsberg, William A. Frosch, and Theodore Shapiro. Reprinted from the *Archives of General Psychiatry*, 26 (March 1972). Copyright © 1972 by The American Medical Association.

his rights. During the 1950s and especially the 1960s, advances in medical and social science provided the means by which emphasis on equal sexual rights for women has become so important in the 1970s. Women seek and expect orgastic release. Virginity is largely irrelevant. We suggest that these cultural changes have consequences in the structure and manifestations of neurotic phenomena. By breaking the former ecologic balance in society, a disequilibrium has been created, leaving its mark on the male partners of these new women.

Our observations of a group of impotent young men suggest that this cultural trend must be considered as a significant etiologic factor in order to understand their disturbing and anxiety-producing impotence. While impotence has always existed, it now takes on an additional form. Sociologic study is needed to know if there is an absolute increase in the complaint, but clinical psychological study can suggest some avenues for such a sociologic approach. Moreover, clinical study of a manifest symptom provides an avenue to understanding intrapsychic conflict which may earlier have been obscured by socially approved rationalizations. Hartmann et al [1] emphasize that demands of reality prohibit or facilitate drive discharge. While most depth analysis focuses on intrapsychic and familial determinants, the larger social context is also an important factor in falling ill. If it was formerly disregarded, it is only because social changes in this sector occurred more slowly.

The case studies which follow attempt to explore the strain of current social demands upon the psychology and behavior of a group of young men.

CLINICAL DATA

CASE 1.—A 19-year-old college student complained that fear of losing his erection had resulted in severe social inhibition with women. Following a period of pleasurable sexuality which included petting, his girl friend had suggested that their sexual practices were immature and that coitus was more appropriate. He ejaculated prematurely and then was impotent. He had formerly been more comfortable in his voyeurism because "the female is never responsible for compliance, for she doesn't even realize I am looking." Masturbation or fellatio was acceptable because "my penis is the center of attention" and he did not feel "used and appreciated as a tool." Coitus is difficult because he sees it as "doing something for her"; he had been potent when he did not feel "compelled to continue [to coitus] by social pressure," when he is reassured that he is cared for and when he feels loved. He did not, however, find it easy to give love.

CASE 2.—A man in his mid-30s was referred for therapy after

urologic examination had failed to reveal any organic basis for his impotence. He sought both consultations because his wife threatened divorce: she was unsatisfied by sexual practices limited to foreplay. The patient felt that his problems resulted from lack of experience. Driven to excel in order to impress his powerful and effective father, he had thrown himself into campus politics and then into the family business. He claimed inadequate time to develop a longer or lasting relationship with a "good girl," one that might have led to sexual involvement. Instead he sought out prostitutes whom he saw as dirty and diseased. Justifying his insistence on fellatio rather than coitus, he said that not only did he thus avoid infection [sic] but he also rationalized it as quicker, permitting prompt return to the major pursuits of his life. He finally married in his early 30s because he felt it was expected of him. Until his wife's insistent demand that he perform sexually, he was able to avoid his anxiety at confronting the female genitals and his own castration anxiety.

CASE 3.—A 24-year-old single white man came for analysis consciously wishing to avoid military service because he was unable to urinate in public toilets. His limited sexual contacts had been marked by impotence or premature ejaculation. His excellent academic performance had deteriorated; he was in danger of not completing his current year of professional school. He lived a monastic existence, and only ventured forth from his cluttered, dirty, shade-drawn apartment to go to work.

He was initially impotent with his fiancee and attempted to drive her away by confessing his difficulties. Her sympathetic and understanding response, at variance with the demanding attitude of other women he had known, allowed him to tolerate the failure. His symptom reflected inhibition of tremendous rage due to his fear of retaliation. He partially gratified both the wish and the defense in not giving the woman what she wanted while protecting himself by refraining. He also preempted the expected retaliation by confession. "How better to take your anger out on a woman—it doesn't matter what the cause is—she has to feel there is something wrong with her—fear will do it, anger will do it [impotence]—but ever since I've been able to love her sex is fun."

CASE 4.—A man in his early 20s entered treatment because of concern about recent impotence. He had met a young woman whom he liked. After the first two dates he felt that she expected him to approach her sexually. When she responded vigorously to his advance, he interrupted with the excuse that her roommate might return. He then felt no longer able to avoid the expected sexual contact and was obliged to invite her to his room. When he attempted coitus he ejaculated immediately after intromission and apologized. A second attempt that same evening ended because he could not sustain an erection. When the failure was repeated on their fourth date his partner suggested there was something wrong and berated him for his failure. In addition, she was unable to achieve orgasm when he tried to practice masturbation on her. She claimed this was unusual and tacitly blamed his insufficiencies. Despite his friends' commiserations concerning her impatience, he became increasingly inhibited, depressed, and aware of his retaliatory rage.

A similar failure in a European brothel at 17 had not been disturbing: he had been able to rationalize that a friend had chosen the prostitute for him and that she was indifferent and mechanical. The psychological features of his current difficulty were the same: although he had not actively chosen to perform, performance was expected, and he did not feel desired "for himself."

COMMENT

Erikson suggested that "social institutions offer ideological rationales for widely different patterns of partial sexual moratoria such as complete sexual abstinence for a specific period, promiscuous genital engagement without personal commitment, or sexual play without genital engagement." [2] This generalization points the way to a consideration of society's role in providing the context for abnormal or unusual behaviors. Ideally we would examine the same individual exposed to varying cultural conditions; the concept of a constant human product with variations in external environment is, however, an abstraction. We can examine clinical variation in symptom profiles over time as an index of the influence of culture on neurotic constellations.

Formerly patients with impotence were, for the most part, married men who gradually began to withdraw sexually from their wives following a period of more successful sexual functioning. They complained that the excitement had passed and that their wives no longer provided the variety in sexual practices they craved. Impotence was accompanied by minimal anxiety: they usually had conscious fantasies about the secretary at work, the girl next door, etc., and felt confident that novel objects or practices could revive their interest. This conviction prevented the emergence of major anxiety and resulted in relative indifference to their wives' plaints. Indeed, there was often either a kind of hysterical belle indifference or hostility toward the spouse. One of our patients (not cited in this paper) did succumb to a readily available partner. The temptation exceeded the restraining limits of fantasy satisfactions and he was impotent with this new and presumably exciting partner.

A second type of impotence accompanied by more anxiety is seen in younger men of borderline disposition or with a large component of latent homosexual or polymorphously perverse attitudes. Hostility to women and a strong degree of castration anxiety mark the underpinnings of their personality. One of our patients (case 2) with such problems was able to postpone any awareness of his coital inhibitions for many years. His wife's demands led to the loss of his rationalizations and development of anxiety.

Currently young men describe failures occurring early in their relationships. Following such early failure they become preoccupied with its meaning to their manhood. They either withdraw or, more characteristically, venture into counterphobic attempts to regain self-respect. Patient 4 represents this counterphobic choice. While it did not result in Don Juanism with repetitive failure, humiliation and lowering of self-esteem did occur. Anxiety sometimes leads to commiseration with friends or, if the female partner is tolerant, a "stiff upper lip" feminine forbearance provides the male with a patient mother —vintage 1971 (case 3). Accompanying drug use may contribute to the failure or be used to rationalize it.

When we explored these sexual failures occurring early in a relationship, we found a common male complaint: these newly freed women demanded sexual performance. The male concern of the 1940s and 1950s was to satisfy the woman. In the late 1960s and early 1970s, it seems to be "will I have to maintain an erection to maintain a relationship?" This idea is permeated with feelings of "who calls the shots" and "who is sex for." There is a reversal of former roles: the role of the put-upon Victorian woman is that of the put-upon man of the 1970s. "Whereas a man's impotence is obvious, a woman's frigidity can be hidden." [3] Inhibited nonorgastic women can often hide their lack of response but men without erect penises cannot even feign intromission. This challenge to manhood is most apparent in a sexually liberated society where women are not merely available but are perceived as demanding satisfaction from masculine performance.

Such newly free women might say, "So be it—let the chips fall where they may." Women's sense of exploitation, however, often results in retaliatory rage and distortion of many worthwhile libertarian and equalizing aims. Unconscious transmission of feminine revenge by an aggressive manner and overassertiveness may enhance a man's castration anxiety with consequent fear of the vagina. This must be seen in an adaptational and social framework rather than as a purely psychological and particularly intrapsychic phenomenon.

Kubie has suggested, "A free society does not automatically bring psychological freedom to the individual; but it makes it possible for him to strive for it." [4] Although for some the new "sexual freedom" may indeed be liberating, for others it merely induces different symptoms rather than improved mental health. Although focused on the decreased control of aggression rather than on sexual symptomatology, a recent paper states that "sexual freedom has, in accordance with Freud's conception of repression, considerably transformed the manifestations of the neuroses; . . . [it has produced] . . . new neurotic constellations. . . . The task of 'reconciling men to civilization' is not made easier through the liberation of drives." [5]

REFERENCES

1. Hartmann H, Kris E, Loewenstein RM: Some psychoanalytic comments on "culture and personality," in Wilbur G, Muensterberger W (eds): *Psychoanalysis and Culture*. New York, International Universities Press, 1951, pp 3–31.

2. Erikson EH: *Identity, Youth and Crisis*. New York, WW Norton & Co Inc Publishers, 1968, p 187.

3. Fenichel O: *The Psychoanalytic Theory of Neurosis*. New York, WW Norton & Co Inc Publishers, 1945, p 174.

4. Kubie L: *Psychoanalysis and Contemporary Science*. New York, Macmillan Co Publishers, to be published.

5. Lowenfeld H, Lowenfeld Y: Our permissive society and the superego: Some current thoughts about Freud's cultural concepts. *Psychoanal Quart* 39:607, 1970.

the feminization of the american male

Dotson Rader

Several weeks ago I attended a "men's liberation" session in New York. The group was composed of seven married men who met each week for "consciousness raising" in an attempt to cope with their tortured relationships with women. They drew the following conclusions: both men and women are sexually oppressed; men are coerced from an early age into playing dishonest sexual and social roles; they were "feminized." One of the liberation group members said, "We're taught in school not to act like boys but like little emasculated adults. Sit quiet! Don't talk! Be neat! We're made to act like little girls! In high school and college we're treated like minors, although we're functioning sexually as men. In high school, you know, you have to get a written slip from a teacher to go to the bathroom! And you're *eighteen years old!* Man! And once we're married we are trapped into other false, emasculating roles. You just can't win. You're supposed to be tough like John Wayne, and when you try that number, they knock you down. It's a hell of a mess."

It is indeed. It is enormously difficult for young men to even survive manhood in the United States. The situation is bad and it is getting *worse*. Apparently, for the first time, impotence is a significant problem among some young males. Males account for seventy per cent of all suicides. Over eighty per cent of chronic alcoholics are male, as are ninety-seven per cent of convicted felons. The abandonment and divorce rate among all population groups is at an all-time high. Competent observers report that the incidence of homosexuality among males under thirty has increased dramatically in the last decade, as has male addiction to hard drugs. Patricia Sexton, in *Psychology Today,* reports that one out of every four boys fails in school. In some New York high schools the dropout rate among males approaches seventy per cent in the senior year. Certainly the most frightening tendency is the rampant increase in crimes of violence by young males. Murder, rape, assault and gratuitous violence, whether by individual youths or by gangs of boys, are indicative of the frustration and despair of males in American society. I think that much student rebellion, crime, family abandonment, school and job failure are directly related to the emasculation of the male.

The young male has difficulty in establishing his manhood (sense of personhood as a male) because he has few constructive outlets for his aggression and because of a profound confusion in sexual role and identity. And that confusion, I submit, is the result of the early attempts to "feminize" the boy. Little distinction is drawn between the significant inherent differences in physical and mental ability of boys and girls. Boys are subjected, from infancy on, to predominantly feminine influences which result in the enforcement of "feminine" values. By "feminine values" (an ambiguous term at best) I mean passivity, neatness, quietness, mannerliness, obedience and the expression of aggression through verbal rather than physical devices (speech rather than fists).

Because of the growing abandonment of families by black males, and the decades-old abandonment of parental responsibility by middle- and upper-class males, many boy children are raised by women. In school they are generally taught by women who comprise eighty-five per cent of all elementary school teachers. Without an adequate male presence in the home and school, boys are denied adult male figures to emulate. Thus deprived, boys turn to peer group aggregates—other boys—to learn what it means to be male.

This "feminization" of the young male's world leads to the creation of values which are contrary and resistant to adult values. Authority—always presented in the form of a woman—drives boys, by nature rebellious to authority, to hostility to women. This hostility, soon internalized, prevents a man from becoming whole and results in antisocial and self-destructive behavior.

We have been too hard on men. We have demanded too much of them. It is time someone spoke out in their behalf.

It is a fact: men are *weaker* than women. Men are less capable of surviving sustained anxiety, and yet we teach them that their manhood depends on competitive strength and on competence in administrative and executive tasks. And we know the grim results. Men die an average of seven years earlier than women. They suffer fifty-eight per cent of disabling accidents. They have dramatically higher rates of alcohol and drug addiction, suicide, and preadult behavioral disorder. Even as babies men are weaker: 135 boys are born dead for every 100 girls; male babies are miscarried twice as often as girl babies; fifty-four per cent more boy infants than girls are injured at birth. Girls are tougher than boys. Girls are eighteen months ahead in physical maturity, and until the last year of high school they consistently outperform boys on all written achievement tests.

What we must do is *decrease* the pressure on men to compete and master; *increase* their freedom of spontaneous action and healthy aggression; and end their captivity to women in the early years when sexual identity, manners and role playing are learned.

The cause of much degradation and emasculation is American coeducation: that is where male failure begins and where it is institutionalized. In coeducational schools, boys are placed in situations where they are forced to compete for grades and adult attention with girls. They invariably lose, for they are behind girls in physical and intellectual development: they have inferior fine muscle control (which makes writing more difficult for them); and they have twice the speech difficulty of girls (four times as many boys stutter as girls). In American coeducational schools the academic disciplines are sexualized. Those which have immediate value to the national industrial economy and defense are deemed "masculine." Boys are expected to excel in them, girls are not. Mathematics, science, history, manual and industrial trades are the province of boys. Poetry, English, "home economics," music and art are the areas "appropriate" for girls. Boys who do well in these areas and not in the "male" subjects are usually thought of as "sissies" by their peers. This attitude is not only detrimental to the development of manhood but also to society. Competitive sports, the primary tools for the training in martial skills, are consigned to young males. It is here that the fiercest pressure is applied to boys, whether on the school playing fields or in other adult-structured sports situations (like the Little League). It is here that the cruel distortion of masculinity is most clearly seen. Boys grow up believing that their manly competence depends on athletic performance. Later, sex itself becomes a kind of sport in which manhood is tested and abused; dehumanizing games are played which have no real connection with masculinity. Through the sexualization of disciplines, the coeducational system traps children in a constrictive pattern of socially and politically determined sexual roles.

In part, the New Left is a reaction against the conformity to "feminine values," to emasculation. Homosexuality is, by definition, a rejection of women; perhaps male violence is also a rejection. I think the Weatherman in macho clothes, the bikers in butch poses and the super-tough young men in ultra-masculine postures are sexually insecure. They are attempting to reject childhood feminization by positing a militant, if caricatured, masculinity in its place.

It is vital to restore a healthy sense of American manhood. How can we do this? We should abolish coeducation up to the senior high school year. We must get over the notion that learning is a competitive chore, that democratic ideals require that boys and girls be treated in the same fashion. We should encourage and support boys' clubs and teams, for these groupings reinforce feelings of male independence and competence. Boys should be apprenticed to adult males at an early age and taught a manual trade that will awaken feelings of physical adequacy and autonomy. It is important that boys and older males be allowed a continuity of social interplay.

Finally, I believe that the adoption of children by single males should be legalized, and that the automatic right of mothers to the custody of children in divorce actions be ended. Children in fatherless homes should be given a male foster parent or placed in day care centers staffed by men.

If we are to halt the increasing impotence and failure of the American male, we must abolish the codes, institutions and practices which lead to the frustration and feminization of young boys. If our culture, which has so distorted their manhood, refuses to change, young men will continue to retaliate with violence and social destructiveness.

Chapter 15

the transexual metamorphosis

Elaine Louie

"Choose between a very unhappy homosexual boy or a reasonably happy girl." So says Harry Benjamin, M.D., the eighty-eight-year-old geriatrician and practitioner in sexology, who first introduced the term transexual to the Academy of Medicine in New York City twenty-one years ago, and made the then-alarming statement: "If you can't change the mind to fit the body, change the body to fit the mind."

The transexual is the person whose physical and psychic sex are opposed. Today, the transexual doesn't have to be at war with himself. Surgery can unite the mind and body. Although the Emperor Nero may have ordered one of the earliest sex-change operations on a young male exslave, and another Roman emperor, Heliogabalus, supposedly married a slave and then took up the tasks of a wife, offering half the Roman Empire to the physician who could give him female genitalia, cosmetically acceptable conversion surgery is recent.

Nor has it been perfected. A functioning but obviously non-ovulating set of female sexual organs can be created, but the phallic reconstruction, complete with testes and scrotum, doesn't urinate, ejaculate, or erect (without the help of a thin plastic rod). Yet forty institutions do operate, and innumerable transexuals have found the surgical path to a new life. Of these, men outnumber women four to one. And some of these people come to Stanford University's Gender Identity Program in Palo Alto, California, where I first learned that the transexual is not a social leper. He has a medical disease.

Doctors believe that transexualism is often based on a hormonal disturbance that occurs *in utero,* possibly from hormones administered to the pregnant mother. Since the hormonal component can't be detected in an adult, doctors are trying to discover transexual behavior early in life. Devices include chromosomal identification, careful histories of hormone treatment to the mother, and (in the work of Dr. Richard Green, psychiatrist and head of U.C.L.A.'s Gender Identity Research and Treatment Clinic) work with nearly a dozen children, some as young as three, who already show signs of what may be transexual behavior. As Dr. Norman Fisk, the relaxed, open-faced psychiatrist at Stanford puts it, "If you catch it early, there's no need to patch it up, as it were, in life."

Hormones, however, aren't the only cause. A transexual may have had a wrong upbringing. Pat Gandy, the administrator of Stanford's Gender Identity Program, reports that a psychotic mother reared two males as girls, and Dr. Benjamin heard of a Chinese family in which two boys were brought up as girls. Sitting in an easy chair in his hotel suite, he muses aloud: "Wouldn't it be strange that a Chinese mother and father would bring up a boy as a girl since the Chinese have traditionally favored the son?"

Transexuals are all races, ages, classes, and occupations. Stanford has had a physicist as well as clerks. Apparent misfits to the straights, transexuals are united by their feeling that their real sex is not their anatomical sex. But that's not how the parent usually sees it.

"My son, the woman" is no joke to any parent. "When that doctor says at birth, 'That's a boy'—or 'that's a girl'—it really sticks," says Fisk, who's interviewed every transexual at Stanford since 1968. "And it's very hard for the parent to recognize their child is a transexual."

"He's a boy, a boy, a boy! For me, he's a boy!" says the mother of a transexual male-to-female, a few months before the operation but a year after hormone treatment began. Breasts, silky face, and even forthcoming vagina aside, because she knew him as a boy, she sees him as a son.

Slowly, most of the families become understanding, though it may be expressed cynically. Stanford had one father who brought in his son with the resigned but acerbic comment: "I'd rather have a daughter than a faggot son."

Others are more positive. According to Dr. Benjamin, Christine Jorgensen's parents say of their celebrated daughter: "Christine is our *child*—it doesn't make a difference if she's a boy or girl. She's our child." (Jorgensen, who is now forty-six, lives in Long Beach, California, traveling and lecturing in colleges. Dr. Benjamin, who is a personal friend of Jorgensen's and saw her in 1973, says, "Christine is a lovely, normally feeling woman.")

Occasionally, brothers and sisters are also affected. One transexual's brother used to get his kicks by going to New York's West Village and punching the queens. Today, confronted with his own brother, he must be at least slightly astonished. Maybe even ashamed. But the family history is just part of Stanford's criteria for choosing the successful candidate for surgery. (Those who are denied surgery are offered continued hormone treatment and behavior modification, however.)

In a slight Southern drawl, Pat Gandy says, "We also ask about the candidate's own sexuality, particularly penile pleasure." Transexuals don't consider themselves homosexual. One complained bitterly of homosexual love-making. "Immediately he'll feel my penis, make sure I'll have an erection, which will turn *him* on and *me* off." Worse, the transexual might be asked to bang his partner. This is catastrophic.

Although the transexual wants the operation to turn his life-long fantasy into a reality, he's also prone to illusions—including one of massive orgasms.

"Our patients do climax—not all of them all of the time," says Dr. Charles Ihlenfeld, the young, soft-spoken endocrinologist and associate of Dr. Benjamin's. "It takes longer. They can build sexual tension in their bodies, ears, neck, and release it pleasurably." He stops and thinks a minute. "Orgasm, at least to me, is physical." But for the transexual, it may be more psychological and emotional. Gandy says that over half their patients who've been followed up state they do have orgasms. "But we haven't taken anyone to Masters and Johnson so we don't know if they have the equivalent of the female orgasm." Doctors assume that the transexual's orgasm is primarily psychological and emotional. Curious, though, I ask Dr. Benjamin if the transexual might be an extraordinary lover since she's been both sexes. He chuckles quietly, eyes twinkling. "I've heard *that* one before!"

"Some have the illusion of becoming a star or that suddenly the world will open, and job offers will come pouring in," Gandy continues. Laughing, he tells the story of one wishfully thinking young woman. "She thought after surgery she was going to meet a man straight out of the pages of *Gentleman's Quarterly*—and that he would take care of her for the rest of her life . . . well, she *did!* She *found* him! She lived with him for a couple of days, she was so turned on, but, according to her—he was so super-straight, and of course the surgery wasn't perfect, that he'd ask about her anatomy and she was constantly having to lie and hide. Finally, she said, 'People from *Gentleman's Quarterly* just aren't the sort of people I want!'"

Although the initial interview explores the candidate's relationships to family, friends, and lovers, success in the chosen gender role and work is the most important criteria for surgery. Does she pass?

"By success, we don't mean being a highly paid, highly successful writer for a magazine," warns Gandy. Consistent with medical thinking, success means within a realistic, nonillusory society. "If a patient is working and passing as a female clerk at Woolworth's, and she's going out to work every day—that's success."

If Gandy thinks the candidate is good, he refers him or her to Dr. Fisk for a two-hour observation, full endocrinological work-up, and psychiatric testing. Fisk, who saw his "first woman with male organs" in 1968, administers the 440-question MMPI (Minnesota Multiphasic Personality Inventory) test, which has a male and female rating. "And we give a strong vocational index."

Since 1968, he's been able to elicit greater candor from the patients. "The first candidate had the 'perfect' classic Benjaminian history, including cross-dressing and a lifelong history, dating from birth, of wanting to be the other sex. In fact," Fisk says, "all the patients we saw in the first year and a half were classic Benjaminian. It was very frustrating, and we knew it wasn't so." Transexuals were so eager to have the surgery they simply memorized Dr. Benjamin's book, *The Transexual Phenomenon*.

"There are other criteria," Fisk tells me, "where a transvestite moves into transexualism or they've even been married and fathered children. Therefore, we don't rely a lot on psychological testing. If the testing confirms our clinical impression that's useful. Sometimes the testing may contradict." Since the most important index is "passing," Stanford asks that they live for at least a year in the role of choice before surgery.

Transexuals also have private and group psychiatric therapy by the entire staff of twenty doctors, administrators, nurses, social workers, and former patients. Further, there's behavior modification.

A professional model and voice expert teach the patients makeup, how to fix the hair, how to dress, how to sit, and how to shake hands so the hand held out doesn't look like a broken wrist. The bone-crunching handshake is also avoided. Table etiquette includes learning how to hold the utensils, and a voice expert shows them how to raise the tone and the inflection in their voices.

There are few women staff members in Stanford's program. Nurses, models, and voice experts may be women, but no surgeons or psychiatrists. Gandy says, "I suppose that because so few women are encouraged to become surgeons or psychiatrists that we reflect the fact that women are often cultural victims. But we'd be glad to have a woman surgeon—or psychiatrist."

Although surgery is liberating for the transexual, that sense of freedom is not related to women's liberation. "They are more female than females," says Dr. Fisk. "They want to be traditional housewives and mothers. But put traditional in quotation marks."

The majority of transexuals want the heterosexual relationship completely, but there are exceptions. A male transexual may become attracted to women for the first time in his life. "Or two people, a man happily married to a woman, where they loved each other, sex aside, as people, but wanted to live together as two women," Fisk reports. "This was our first patient to change sex in order to pursue a homosexual relationship." He offers a psychological explanation: "If a transvestite gets involved with a latent homosexual, as her homosexuality becomes more overt, the transvestite must change to transexual in order to save the relationship."

Surgery may free the transexual to relate more easily to both sexes. "For the male who used to fear women, once the penis is gone he can now relate to women because he has nothing to fear. And because men are so cruel to feminine males, it's hard for the transexual to have sexual/love relations with a man."

I ask if Lesbians were asking for surgery since women's and gay lib have taken hold. Both Gandy and Fisk say no. Gandy answers, "I talk to Lesbians alone, not as couples, at first, because they are often terrified that their relationship will be destroyed by surgery and that they're moving towards the more normally acceptable male/female relationship. Threatened Lesbians are emphatically opposed to being transexuals . . . as personally and emotionally threatened as heterosexual men by the surgery."

Once surgery is approved, the law steps in. The operation is never performed without the patient's written consent, witnessed by an attorney. The male-to-female conversion is essentially irreversible, and the female-to-male transexual can't have back her vagina without great difficulty and scarring.

Asked how he arranges for document changes for the patients, Gandy answers, "Very quietly." "Although the law should make a place for people to make their new lives easy," says Dr. Benjamin, "the law moves very very slowly and makes it very difficult. The patients go elsewhere, or they avoid as much as possible, and we tell them just to get as many documentations as possible." Driver's licenses, birth certificates, Social Security cards, school transcripts, charge accounts, and passports can all be changed to a new name.

The surgery itself is extremely painful. For the male-to-female conversion, doctors remove the testicular organs and erectile tissue within the penis, and make the female organs from the penile skin, scrotal skin, and secondary skin tissue. (Dr. Georges Burou of Morocco fashions the vagina from skin stripped off the penis. But this procedure is extremely delicate as the stripped skin can bruise easily.) A split-thickness skin graft, usually taken from the thighs or buttocks, lines the vagina. The urethra is displaced so the patient can urinate downward like a woman, and the scrotal skin makes up the labia majora and minora.

The female-to-male patient receives from skin graft a cosmetically acceptable penis—complete with scrotum and testes—that other men and many women assume is real, but it doesn't function as a penis.

"As a sexual organ, though, it works very well," says Fisk. "For the first year, since it's made out of skin grafts, the penis *is* rigid. After, he can insert a plastic rod, which becomes invisible, for rigidity." Apparently, their female partners haven't noticed. "I guess our patients turn off the lights before insertion or tell them they had an injury in the war," Fisk speculates, "and I understand there is also some sensation." But this conversion is not just a series of complex operations. The operations may succeed but the overall results are still somewhat doubtful. Therefore, not many female transexuals actually have a penis made, although they do have a mastectomy and hysterectomy besides hormone treatments. "Sometimes the androgen treatment increases the size of the clitoris," says Dr. Benjamin, "and sometimes it becomes a little penis." He indicates a measurement of approximately three and a half inches. "The book on female transexuals has yet to be written because doctors are still working on how to perfect the penis."

The staff decides the operating procedure long in advance of the actual operating date, but the twenty-four-hour pre-op procedure of chemical tests and bowel preparation might necessitate changes in the scheduling. "Chemical tests may change medication, or anything may happen to the scheduling which will postpone the operation. There might be an emergency, beds may be filled, and some patients can't handle preoperative stress." He sighs. "We just prepare them as best as possible."

Now, the surgery itself. The patient lies supine, with hypotensive anesthesia carefully administered so the surgeon has a relatively dry field for accurate visualization in order to avoid entering the bladder, urethra, or rectum. Skin grafts are also taken at this point.

Then the patient is placed, knees raised, so the two-by-seven-inch stent can be inserted, covered by the skin graft. As indicated, scrotal skin becomes the labia majora and minora, and the penile skin "is" the clitoris. Postoperatively, patients are told to expect pain, although not all do. Certainly they are weak and numb. For seven days, their legs are completely wrapped together and feeding is intravenous, a catheter inserted for urination, and the stent placed inside the vagina to keep it open.

"Sometimes there's a postoperative depression for one to two weeks," says Gandy, "because the patient is coming out of anesthesia and the body's been attacked." One patient looked at her vagina for the first time and said, "I paid $4,000 for *this?*" (Prices vary abroad and in the United States, from $2,500 to $7,500.)

Stanford advises the patient to wear the stent for three months to prevent the vagina from closing. But the happy transexual hardly minds.

After surgery, the operated transexual can be highly promiscuous. "People prior to hormone treatment and possible surgery are relatively inhibited in their new role," says Ihlenfeld, "but after surgery they're discovering themselves and often sleep with anybody who'll go to bed with them, to get the acceptance that they're women. Eventually, they quiet down and find a partner who's suitable for them."

And most marry quietly. Transexuals, by and large, do not shout from the rooftops, "Hey, look at me!" They wish to forget. "They get married and never tell their partner they had a gender problem, and some who are unstable in their life-style move around," says Gandy, admitting that although his follow-up program is probably the best, it's not good. For the transexuals, however, denying the past isn't as great a burden as one might think. Their inner reality had been denied before.

androgyny—our
future humanhood

According to an ancient myth recorded by Euripides and Plato and found in other, non-Western cultures, the original human was neither male nor female. The primal human was at once both male and female, capable of self-impregnation, complete, and self-fertile in its own psyche and body. But then, as a punishment for some mysterious crime, this primal human was split into two components: "male and female He made them." Ever since, the two human halves have struggled with varying success to regain the lost unity of Eden. Our "agonizing search for this lost androgynous unity is," in the view of psychologist Ignace Lepp, "what we call love."

Endless debates and discussions can be devoted to the myths and realities of psychophysical symbiosis—the psychological and physical complementarity of the human male and female. We could also delve into the *anima* and *animus* archetypes proposed by Jungian psychology. Jung's theory of compensation, which maintains that men and women are infinitely more complementary than opposed because each is a mixture of what any one society may label masculine and feminine traits, is certainly relevant to our conclusion here. We could also explore the results of modern research on human sexual and gender differentiation. This latter study would lead us to conclude, in the words of Dr. John Money, director of the Johns Hopkins Gender Indentification Clinic, that "there is as much difference between one man and another, or between one woman and another, as there is between a man and a woman."

Whatever its historical roots may be, androgyny is a radical view of the human species. Its potential repercussions are at once devastating and pregnant with new, rich insights into the potential of our evolving humanhood.

In the first essay in this concluding section, Carolyn Heilbrun lucidly explores the real meaning of androgyny as it goes beyond the feminist movement hopefully to creatively depolarize the sexes. An androgynous culture, she predicts, will resolve the destructive role conflicts which have restricted personal growth so heavily in our culture. Heilbrun details the meaning of androgyny as revealed in the heroes and heroines of literature, past and contemporary. In the second essay, Linda Barufaldi and Emily Culpepper discuss "the radical madness" inherent in androgyny. They see in this view of personhood a vital new potential for human flexibility and growth. In terms of sexual relationships, they see a shift in consciousness and behavior which may very well make the 1970s the Decade of Bisexuality, as some noted futurists and family sociologists predict. Finally, in a one-sentence overview of the future of sexual relations, Jean Rostand, the visionary biologist and son of the creator of Cyrano de Bergerac, gives us a glimpse of what androgyny may mean for our future as biological organisms who control and design their modalities of reproduction and genetic constitutions. This single sentence returns us full circle to the technologies which so many people rightly fear as the trigger for a major revolution in the future relations of men and women.

Chapter 16

recognizing the androgynous human

Carolyn G. Heilbrun

The idea of androgyny apparently takes a little getting used to. The word is not yet either familiar or comfortable, and those who have not given much thought to the matter tend to respond either with bewilderment or hostility. When I wrote my book, *Toward a Recognition of Androgyny,* I thought, in my innocence, that I could give the word's etymology, round it off with a few caveats, and go on to a discussion of the central idea. The months since its publication have taught me that the word has become both more and less threatening than I had anticipated.

The etymology is simple enough. *Androgyny* comprises two Greek words: *andros,* man, and *gyne,* woman. There is no logical reason why the compound could not be reversed so that the root word for woman came first. There is, in fact, a word, gynandromorph, which means the same thing, but this seems to be one of those cases in which discussions about precedence must give way before the simple demands of sound.

If you look *androgyny* up in a dictionary, you will probably find that the definition for it is hermaphrodite, an individual who has both male and female sex organs. Naturally, neither I nor anyone else interested in the concept of androgyny uses the word in this way. Hermaphroditism is a physical anomaly among higher animals and humans, unconnected with any of my ideas of androgyny. If, next, you spring the word *androgyny* on someone generally intelligent but uninformed in this matter, he or she will probably decide that the word means bisexual—that is, capable of sexual relations and satisfaction with either men or women, both homosexual and heterosexual relations. There is no doubt that as we learn more and more about people's lives, we discover that far more people were and are bisexual than we might have thought, and I suspect that this is an idea with which we are going to have to sit more comfortably in years to come. But it hasn't to do with what I mean by androgyny.

Androgyny, as I mean the word and as it is passing into wider usage, is a human condition in which one behaves in such a way as to indicate a balance of those characteristics we have labelled "masculine": rationality, aggressiveness, courage, energy; and those we have labelled "feminine": gentleness, patience, passivity, intuitiveness. This use of the word grows out of the meaning it had for writers like Coleridge and Virginia Woolf, who knew that if individuals cannot use both the "masculine" and "feminine" parts of their brain, they cannot be artists, great minds, or truly imaginative individuals. Those who use only one part of their brain begin, if I may speak metaphorically, as quarterbacks or cheerleaders, and end as corporation managers or corporation managers' wives. Such people are imprisoned at one end or the other of the spectrum of human possibility.

Let me offer one or two examples of how the word *androgyny* as I use it is passing into general usage. Dr. Mary P. Rowe, an economist at MIT, delivered an address recently on androgyny in the celebration of MIT's one-hundredth year since admitting its first woman student. In a subsequent interview with the *Christian Science Monitor,* she asked pointed and practical questions: Why can't men cry if they want to and join the nurturant professions, caring for children and those who are ill? Why can't women be innovative and financially independent? She pointed out that her generation of women, like mine, was taught to fear success in paid employment and encouraged in dependency, while at the same time men identified the dependence of women and their own refusal to take daily part in the raising of children with something they called manliness. Now, Dr. Rowe suggests, "men must learn their options to sing, to decorate, to garden, to play, to cry, to open up huge areas of self once blocked off," while women must escape from their isolation of housework, from their low self-esteem, from their drive toward denial of the self.

My second example is more technical and revolutionary. Psychiatry is beginning to some extent to free itself from its Freudian strictures concerning the development of core gender identity. It is beginning to perceive gender as a phenomenon with strong cultural determinants by no means exclusively dependent on anatomy. A recent study goes so far as to demonstrate that where sexual polarization exists in young children, it is those children who resist sexual polarization and tend toward androgyny who are most likely to develop into mature adults.

Let me explain this in a little more detail. Jeanne Humphrey Block, of the Institute of Human Development at the University of California, Berkeley, has described a study which traced the "development of sex-role definition, [relating it to] ego and cognitive development and the forces for socialization which derive from parents and culture." Sexual polarization, this study shows, begins at about the age of five, when "a critical bifurcation in the sex role development of boys and girls occurs. Socialization patterns impinge differently on the two sexes: boys are encouraged to control affect, while girls are encouraged to control aggression." By the time of the highest level of ego functioning is reached, when the individual has evolved for himself or herself an identity consonant with history and aspiration, this identity will, ideally, represent an integration of masculine and feminine traits and values. Such a sex-role definition Dr. Block calls androgynous.

Dr. Block studied sex stereotypes in six countries, Norway, Sweden, Denmark, Finland, England, and the United States. Significantly greater emphasis was placed on early and clear sex typing in America than in any other country she studied, and less emphasis was placed in America upon the control of aggression in males. It was the ultimate point of the study that the more androgynous the individual, the higher his or her level of maturity. It followed, therefore, that "The present American cultural emphasis on masculine machismo and feminine docility appears to impede the development of mature ego functioning." To put this in the context of the kindergarten, if little boys are playing with blocks and engines in one corner and the girls playing with dolls in the other, the likelihood is that the child who resists this sexual stereotyping will grow up to be more mature and intelligent and to function better than those who are content to stay in the block or doll corner exclusively.

The term *androgyny* in the Block study, then, can be seen to mean a resistance to sexual polarization. I welcome this because I perceive sexual polarization, a clinging to the received ideas of "masculine" and "feminine," to be destructive in three major ways. First, we lock individuals into prisons of gender where their response is likely to be either mindless acquiescence or violence and rebellion. Second, we deprive both men and women of their common humanity in relation to one another and, in our popular culture at least, emphasize more the war between the sexes than their commonality; except during mating, man and woman are seen as adversaries. Finally, sexual polarization greatly endangers our own survival by placing in power those men at the most "masculine" end of the spectrum of human possibility. In my book, I wrote of the danger of developing in men the ideal "masculine" characteristics of competitiveness, aggressiveness, and defensiveness, and of placing in power those men who most embody these traits. Unless we can effectively check the power of manly men and the women who willingly support them, we will experience new Vietnams, My Lais, and Kent States [cf. Leonard, p. 28]. The animal world is now threatened by the aggression of man, the hunter. So long as we continue to believe that the "feminine" qualities of gentleness, lovingness, and the counting of cost in human (rather than national or property) terms are out of place among rulers, we can look forward to continued self-brutalization and perhaps even to self-destruction. When I first drafted that passage for the book, the Watergate scandals had not yet flared up to illuminate the character of our national leadership. I will confine myself merely to noting the devotion to sexual polarization and nonandrogyny on the part of all those associated with our present federal administration. A less androgynous crew it would be impossible to collect, or even imagine.

If I say that androgyny suggests a spirit of reconciliation between the sexes; suggests a full range of experience open to individuals who may, as women, be aggressive, or, as men, tender; suggests a spectrum upon which human beings choose their places without regard to propriety or custom; I have defined a cultural ideal. But it is helpful to examine how this ideal has been and is being translated in our literature, past and present.

Androgyny is connected to the study of literature in at least three ways which I would like to touch on. The first way concerns itself with what is virtually a new reading of familiar literature. Whether we realize it or not—and each day more of us are coming to realize it —we have read literature as though we were all men in a male-centered universe. Not only have we arbitrarily equated male with fully human, so that it has often not occurred to us that women might be the moral center of literature—we have tended to judge the moral energy of female characters in connection with some conventional idea of female propriety.

Here, for example, is Lionel Trilling's comment:

Women in fiction only rarely have the peculiar reality of the moral life that self-love bestows. Most commonly they exist in a moon-like way, shining by the reflected moral life of men. They are "convincing" or "real" and sometimes "delightful," but they seldom exist as men exist— as genuine moral destinies. We do not take note of this; we are so used to the reflected quality that we do not observe it. . . . Nor can we say that novels are deficient in realism when they present women as they do: it is the presumption of our society that women's moral life is not as men's. No change in the modern theory of the sexes, no advances in status that women have made, can contradict this. The self-love that we do countenance in women is of a limited and passive kind, and we are troubled if their self-love is as assertive as man's is permitted, and expected, to be. Not men alone, but women as well, insist on this limitation, not simply, and not without qualification and exception, not without pleasure when the exception appears, but in general and with the quiet effectiveness of an unrealized, unconscious intention.

Now the androgynous view of literature enables us to see women not as moon-like, shining by the reflected moral life of men, but themselves embodying the central energy of the work. It is an extraordinary fact, for example, how often in the English novel the moral burden of the work is borne by a woman. If we omit the Fielding, Dickens, and Conrad tradition, do we not find that most major English novelists have in fact placed their female heroes in the central position? Let me simply name some of these major English novelists: Defoe, Richardson, Jane Austen, Charlotte and Emily Brontë, George Eliot, Thackeray, Trollope, Henry James, Lawrence, Woolf, and Forster. Noticing the centrality of female characters, we are able then to realize that whatever particular moral energy the English novel embodied, that energy is often "feminine" or female, or, to put this differently, women characters often best serve the artistic purpose of the English novelist.

Once we have noticed this fact about the English novel, we need only turn to the American novel to see an extraordinary difference. With the single exception of *The Scarlet Letter,* American fiction has been a male fiction—the story, as Leslie Fiedler has told us, of two or more men escaping from civilization, where women are, into the wilderness (or onto the sea) where women do not go. We begin to see that there is a connection between the degree of sexual polarization in America, the increasing technocracy and acquisitiveness of our society, and the antiandrogynous quality of our literature.

Having noticed the connection between the centrality of women characters and the quality of the culture which produces the literature we examine, we begin to ask ourselves if, in certain literatures, the male characters may not be more androgynous than we have allowed ourselves to notice. If we take as a standard the unexamined masculinity of most American heroes—the men in Dickey's *Deliverance* will do for starters, those men who hunt one another like animals and hunt animals for sport, those men who, having left women behind, rape one another in the wilderness—if we take these men as the standard of the "masculine" in the American novel, we can see how many European authors have, by contrast, embodied in the development of their male characters a sense of the need for the feminine component, that element essential for salvation. The feminine component in Leopold Bloom, in *Ulysses,* is perhaps obvious. But look at Dostoyevsky's *Brothers Karamazov,* or at Thomas Mann's characters in his short stories, Tonio Krueger and, more especially, Ashenbach in *Death in Venice.* Once we have accepted the idea of the androgynous human being, we see Ashenbach's human sin as a denial of the "feminine" within himself. He has allowed his "masculine" rationality and control so to dominate his life, that the "feminine" elements must take their revenge. Think for a moment of the *Bacchae of* Euripides, in which Pentheus repudiates the female followers of Dionysius and is himself destroyed, as is Ashenbach, by those forces he has scorned.

Finally, having taken into account the centrality of female characters and the direct confrontation with androgyny on the part of many central male characters, we can begin to see that much literature we have read in various other ways (and nothing I say necessarily precludes these other interpretations) can be read as a thematic concern with the destructiveness of sexual polarization. Surely it is not chance that the first of the great modern novels, Richardson's *Clarissa*, should have at its center the fatal division of the sexes. Such a division results in much that is destructive to humanity, not least of all an atrophy of sexual life. For women, the sex act becomes equivalent to their loss of selfhood, of identity; for men, it becomes a cruel game, comparable, as Lovelace suggests, to hunting birds. Clarissa proceeds through the experience of rape and betrayal to the wholeness which is represented by Richardson as embodied in the heavenly life. Clarissa triumphs through her death, not in any crude worldly battle, but because she has discovered her spiritual worth and become herself, with a spiritual identity that is almost androgynous in spirit. The principal device Clarissa chooses for her coffin, that of a serpent with its tail in its mouth, is one of the earliest of androgynous symbols. Lovelace and Clarissa begin at the absolute poles of sexual identity. Lovelace, who personifies the male principle, attempts to subdue and dominate without any realization of his own need to be changed, to be overcome.

It has been remarked that while Clarissa, without pretense, tries desperately to refind herself—her phrase for what Lovelace has done to her is to trick her "out of myself"—she is unconsciously attracted to Lovelace and at some level of unawareness desires him sexually. Certainly she does, for she has no wish to isolate herself from the other sex unless she must do so to preserve her very being. From the beginning of the novel, Clarissa would choose the right marriage, the genuine sexual congress, as the highest good life could offer. She chooses to remain single only as an alternative to being used as a thing, as Lovelace and her brother try to use her.

Marvelously portrayed in the novel is Lovelace's fear of giving Clarissa too easy a triumph if he marries her. Aware that he has power and she none—the word *power* is continually emphasized and repeated by Lovelace—he offers reason after reason why he will not, should not, marry Clarissa despite the fact that he is so profoundly drawn to her that marrying her, whom he prefers above all others, might be the obvious course for one who must someday marry in any case. But Lovelace is incapable of offering what cannot be forcibly extracted from him. Had the extreme violence of the patriarchal world not forced Clarissa into his power, he would have had to marry her to obtain her. Once she is in his power, he becomes incapable of generosity or even consideration. The separation of the sexes, with the power all given to the male, corrupts him absolutely. Lovelace, unaware of any feminine impulses in himself, has no source of identification with his powerless victim.

The great evil of the novel is not primarily Lovelace's loss of his feminine self, of which his role as rake is the final rejection. The great evil is the world which disjoins the sexes, forcing them into radically different, even opposing roles, and transforms the sexual impulse to union into a travesty of union, that is, into rape. Uncertain whether Clarissa is an angel or a woman, Lovelace forgets she is a human being, and is doomed. The society which has failed to teach him her humanity stands condemned.

Perhaps Shakespeare can best serve as the other writer in whose works we can discover the theme of androgyny as salvation and the dangers of sexual polarization. From *The Two Gentlemen of Verona,* where a girl disguises herself as a boy, to *The Tempest,* where Ariel, wholly androgynous, quite surpasses any gender delineation, Shakespeare was as devoted to the androgynous ideal as anyone who has ever written. Let us look for a moment at his last plays, which have been called the comedies of forgiveness. In these plays men, by the excessive exercise of their most virile attributes, bring total disaster upon their world, even when, as in *The Winter's Tale,* it is a marvelously happy one; women, who are at first despised and rejected, or ignored, possess the redeeming powers. It is they who make possible the brave new world. And the grace they bring is not aggressively "feminine"; it is the grace of androgyny. That sexual jealousy and lust are so much a masculine creation in the world of, for example, *The Winter's Tale,* is not accidental. The jealousy and lust in these plays signify the failure of sexual union literally and symbolically to manifest itself in an antiandrogynous world. The appealing boy child who dies, in *The Winter's Tale,* with the expulsion of his mother, dies from the lack of the feminine quality in his world. But the lost girl child reappears as redeemer: dressed as Flora in the early scenes in which she appears, Perdita is literally the savior of the world to which she returns, the world shattered by male jealousy reverberating in the extreme state of sexual polarization.

Perhaps you will ask, what is the difference between this androgynous vision of literature and feminist criticism? When all is said and done, have I suggested more to you than a new feminist reading of literature? Naturally, there is a certain amount of similarity between feminism and androgyny, if only because the masculine domination has been so long, so pervasive and so exalted that it is difficult to counteract it without appearing to be remarkably like a feminist in one's discoveries. But the feminist's work is different. She is likely to identify the dangers of stereotyped sex roles in literature, to resurrect those works which speak of women's disabilities and have been submerged, to study a given text exclusively from a modern woman's point of view. She will be interested in the unrecorded documents of women, whether personal or historical, and in awakening her audience to an acute sense of women's powerlessness. Above all, she will be interested in encouraging women to find a voice in which to express their anger, their frustration, their need for autonomy and self-esteem.

I honor all these aims, but they are not quite identical with the aims of those who study and work for androgyny. It is balance, within individuals and within society, that the student of androgyny seeks and, what is subtle and rather hard to identify, he seeks the imaginative embodiment of androgyny where what we know of the author would make us expect to find no such thing. Lawrence is a good example of this. If you read his two essays on the psychology of the unconscious, or some of his later novels, or his critical studies, you would conclude that he was a masculine apologist of the most extreme sort, and you would be right. But if instead you read *The Rainbow* and *Women in Love,* you discover he has endowed female characters with his own experience, and perceived new possibilities for love and self-expression which his didactic works do not account for. As he has taught us, never listen to the teller, listen to the tale.

The androgynous view of literature can see in a male character, like Leopold Bloom in *Ulysses,* or Marcel in Proust's great novel, or Strether in *The Ambassadors,* a new quality which one had not hitherto sought in masculine heroes. This quality suggests a range of experience outside that characterized as "male," and a possibility for new readings of old masterpieces. Perhaps even for new readings of new works.

In the end you may want to say, if you have followed me this far: Fine! But why the word *androgyny?* Why stick to the old categories, why try to yoke so-called male and female characteristics together, instead of calling for what men and women share, which we might call humanity? As someone said to me, ought we not to conceptualize the world in new ways? When we think about androgyny we are still thinking in terms of masculine and feminine. Can't we find new categories, free from the scars of the past? To which my answer would be: I hope we can, I think we must. The best fate for the word *androgyny* would be for it to become meaningless. But, after all, the word *humanity* has been with us a long time, and it has not prevented the fatal stereotyping of which we are all today victims. The sex of an individual is still the first question we ask, the first thing we notice, or try to notice, perhaps the most important fact about an individual, second only to whether he or she is alive or dead. None of us has yet achieved the sensitivity of Chiu-fang Kao in Salinger's short *Taoist Tale.*

Salinger tells of the concerned Duke Mu of Chin whose horse expert was advancing in years and no longer able to travel widely in search of prize stallions and mares for his stables. Queried about a possible replacement, Po Lo noted that "A good horse can be picked out by its general build and appearance. But a superlative horse is something evanescent and fleeting, elusive as thin air." None of Po Lo's sons could discern the elusive qualities of the superlative horse, but Chiu-fang Kao, an old friend and hawker of fuel and vegetables, should be able to fill the position admirably.

Duke Mu hired Chiu-fang Kao and dispatched him in search of a rumored champion steed. Three months passed and Chiu-fang Kao returned with news that he had seen the horse in Shach'iu, a prize dun-colored mare. When the horse finally arrived in Duke Mu's stable, the animal turned out to be a coal-black stallion. Calling Po Lo to task for his poor advice, the Duke complained:

> "That friend of yours, whom I commissioned to look for a horse, has made a fine mess of it. Why, he cannot even distinguish a beast's color or sex! What on earth can he know about horses?" Po Lo heaved a sigh of satisfaction. "Has he really got as far as that?" he cried. "Ah, then he is worth ten thousand of me put together. There is no comparison between us. What Kao keeps in view is the spiritual mechanism. In making sure of the essential, he forgets the homely details; intent on the inward qualities, he loses sight of the external. He sees what he wants to see, and not what he does not want to see. He looks at the things he ought to look at, and neglects those that need not be looked at. So clever a judge of horses is Kao, that he has it in him to judge something better than horses."

I believe we still need the word *androgyny* to shock us into a new understanding of the superlative qualities of something better than horses: human beings as they can be.

Chapter 17

androgyny and the myth of masculine/feminine

Linda L. Barufaldi and Emily E. Culpepper

We are coming to a consciousness of ourselves as androgynous in a culture predicated on the assumption that the physiological differences between females and males are proof of difference in our essential natures. From the moment of birth we have all been taught elaborate complementary definitions of "masculine" and "feminine" identities that radically alter our very awareness of ourselves.

Inherent in this sex-role socialization are two assumptions about sexuality, both of which we reject. First, sexuality is defined solely as a means to an end—procreation—and *not* as a type of relation between persons. This definition implies that our sexuality is expressed only in acts that might ultimately produce the union of an egg and a sperm, and, therefore, that sexual pleasure is not a good in itself. Second, this goal-oriented view of sexuality is used to justify the belief that "normal" sexual relations occur only between one female and one male. The propagation of monogamous heterosexuality as a norm is a primary component of the ideology of the institution of marriage and, consequently, perpetuates the nuclear family. Since the nuclear family is the initial and primary locus of learning and reinforcing sex roles, it is clear that monogamous heterosexuality is a vicious circle.

In realizing the inadequacy of this model of "health," we have begun to recover those aspects of ourselves that were suppressed in conforming to this norm. It is a temptation for us at this point to compensate for the risk and anxiety that accompany nonconformity in our

"Androgyny and the Myth of Masculine/Feminine" by Linda L. Barufaldi and Emily E. Culpepper, copyright © by Linda Barufaldi and Emily Culpepper. Reprinted from *Christianity and Crisis* (April 16, 1973) by permission of the authors.

culture by finding some other model and fixating upon *it*. One obvious temptation is to feel that attraction to one's own sex carries with it the *necessity* to define oneself as exclusively "homosexual." However, this "solution" merely perpetuates the myth that the gender(s) of one's sexual partner(s) is an absolute either/or that becomes definitive of her/his whole life. In short, a theological affirmation of the right to "homosexual" preference is unnecessary because androgynous females and males do not recognize such categories. For this reason, what follows is founded on our intuition and experience of polymorphous sexual Being.

THE MYTHOLOGY OF MASCULINE AND FEMININE

Such an intuition is not easily recovered. Our entire society—family, school, church and state—continually pressures us to believe in the mythology of masculine and feminine. When we are children the message can be very blatant, as in toys and games that teach sex roles. Among adults, this all-pervasive message is more subtly justified by presenting it as if it were the result of an "objective," rational search for knowledge. Consider, for example, Erikson's theory that a sense of inner space is constitutive of female identity, Jung's Amor and Psyche archetypes, Karl Barth's assertion that women are ontologically subordinate to men, or Lionel Tiger's interpretation of male-dominant group behavior as instinctual.

Despite the pervasiveness of such sex-role socialization, we have all experienced some measure of censure and damage for deviation from the norms implicit in these images of "masculine" and "feminine," a fact indicating that these stereotypes do not accurately describe any of us. There is a further contradiction in alleging that these roles are natural in origin while insisting, at the same time, that they be taught and enforced. Our rising self-awareness so radically contradicts our socialization that it annihilates any but the most basic physiological distinctions between female and male. From this perspective we have become painfully conscious of the power these norms continue to have in shaping our lives.

Recently one of us observed two children, a boy about six and a girl about five, in a store with their father. They were of the same height, coloring, facial features and body types, but they looked entirely different. The boy had very short hair, wore a rumpled T-shirt, dungarees and sneakers. The girl had a hairdo with ribbons, a clean, dainty dress and "pretty" shoes that were noticeably uncomfortable. They also behaved very differently. The boy was active and self-assertive; the girl stood around and looked subdued. I found myself staring at them in *horror* as I realized that their pronounced differences were considered normal. I could only wonder what each might have been had each been allowed to develop freely.

These are the children of a world in which we are assigned to one of two prefabricated identities according to our gender. It is grim to learn that gender identity clinics find it easier to alter surgically the sex of a child misidentified at birth (and therefore socially conditioned to be the "wrong" identity) than to enable the child to live as her/his genetically correct sex. A mere acknowledgment of the fact of sex-role conditioning does not fathom the depth and tenacity of its power in us, for surgery is the treatment of choice even for children as young as two years.

Clearly females and males have some different physical experiences (for example, women menstruate and men do not), but the meaning and importance of such phenomena and their effect on personality structure are, at best, unclear, given the extent of patriarchal distortion of our consciousness of them. Since there is so little certainty about the meaning of sex differences and so much evidence of the power of conditioning, speculations about the nature of women and men must be recognized for what they are: working hypotheses.

To describe human behavior as if it were split into two rigid categories is to produce a warped understanding of it. For example, men are taught to cultivate self-assertion to the point of aggression, while women are taught to repress it to such a degree that we sometimes lack this ability almost entirely. In neither sex, therefore, do we find a model for healthy self-assertiveness. From this perspective, it becomes obvious that androgyny cannot consist in "reuniting" (a la Jung, for example) these artificially contrived "halves" called masculine and feminine. Furthermore, the poles masculine and feminine are warped, dualistic configurations that do not describe anything real.

It is not necessary to understand how this has happened to know that it is so. However, it appears to us that this bizarre dualism is an error made in the attempt to comprehend dialectical dynamics in our existence. In the mythology of masculine and feminine these complementary constructs stifle both women and men.

They are also fixed in a hierarchical order. Within the ideology of complementarity those qualities designated as "masculine" (activity, initiative, strength, rationality) are valued more highly than those designated as "feminine" (passivity, receptivity, gentleness, emotion). Moreover, the "masculine" attributes are taken to be the norm since they are the reference points of the males who do the designating. Therefore, the "feminine" attributes come into existence in order to function as the fantasized completion of the "masculine half-person." Thus, we women are defined, and are taught to identify ourselves, as relative to men. This secondary status constitutes a hierarchy with women on the bottom. This is no partnership of equals; it is oppression.

THE NATURE OF ANDROGYNY

As old reality structures have disintegrated, we have become conscious of alternative ways of divining ourselves and our experience. At present we find *androgyny* the most useful way of naming this consciousness. By this we mean that, beyond the specific female and male physical experiences, any human possibility might occur in any of us. Each of us will manifest and develop our own possibility in our own unique way.

No longer confined to a choice between apparently opposite possibilities, we are coming to know ourselves as we are, in flux among many aspects of Being. We discover that reason (formerly considered the province of the male) and intuition (formerly considered the female's province) are both ways of knowing and are not mutually exclusive nor hierarchically ordered. We learn that strength and weakness occur simultaneously in each of us. We create. We improvise. We experiment. We explore. The dimensions of our existence are no longer clearly fixed. We define and discover our own boundaries. A monotonous world of unisex, which would reduce everyone to one mold, is precisely what androgyny is *not*. Androgyny multiplies and celebrates difference.

Relationships are no longer limited to the futile attempts of half-persons to synthesize "masculine" and "feminine" into a single complete being (the "two-become-one" theory). Rather, androgynous relationships exist between and among self-identified females and/or males. Those who understand themselves to be androgynous are capable of many different relationships with either sex.

Lest androgyny sound like a concept to which one could give intellectual assent and be done with it, let us repeat that we are coming to this consciousness of ourselves in a patriarchal society predicated on sexist assumptions. This means that we are experiencing the unfolding of androgynous consciousness as a struggle of liberation. Every time we become more truly who we are, we threaten the sexual caste system that is the foundation of patriarchal civilization. As we love each other, we will inevitably step outside the boundaries patriarchy has imposed on human relationships. Female-with-male relationships lose their static hierarchical meaning. Female-with-female relationship and male-with-male relationship are no longer taboo to us. However, under the patriarchal conditions in which we live, these relationships are illegal, and people participating in them are labeled promiscuous, perverted, sick and sinful. We have no illusions about change coming rapidly. Oppression is deeply damaging and healing is slow.

We struggle to be androgynous knowing that much of our history is lost. Rage fuels our efforts to imagine our past. Much of the history we have had has been lost, burned or distorted. Much of the history we might have had never occurred. The obstacles were too overwhelming. Virginia Woolf tries to imagine what would have happened to a woman who had Shakespeare's genius in Shakespeare's day:

> She was as adventurous, as imaginative, as agog to see the world as he was. But she was not sent to school. She had no chance of learning grammar and logic, let alone of reading Horace and Virgil. She picked up a book now and then. . . . But then her parents came in and told her to mend the stockings or mind the stew and not to moon about with books and papers. . . . Soon, however, before she was out of her teens, she was to be betrothed to the son of a neighboring wool-stapler. She cried out that marriage was hateful to her. . . . The force of her own gift alone drove her to it. . . . She stood at the stage door; she wanted to learn to act, she said. Men laughed in her face. . . . She could get no training in her craft. Could she even seek her dinner in a tavern or roam the streets at midnight?

We carry still within us the unfulfilled promise of these women and of the men who never learned how not to be patriarchs.

A REVOLUTIONARY MADNESS

Over against the prevailing sense of reality, androgyny is anarchy. Patriarchy lives not only in its external social structures but also in our internalized negative self-images as oppressed and oppressor. These images are demons we must find ways to exorcize. To the patriarchal consciousness outside and still within us, we are anathema—our worst nightmares, our wildest fantasies. We are the Enemy we were taught to fear. We say this with a fearsome pride for we realize the enormity of what we are about. We are leaving behind a primary paradigm for domination-subjugation relationships. The very consciousness that constitutes Being is changing.

We find ourselves surviving by paying attention to our basic intuitions—the feelings, imaginings and reflections of our mindbodies. We rely for one source of our strength on this organic awareness of ourselves. We feel less alien as we identify ourselves to each other and as we respond to the androgynous life-energy we find together. It is in this context that we experience healing, thus enabling us not to be defeated by our past.

There remain to be discovered even more ways of making possible the world we are beginning to inhabit. We involve ourselves in concrete struggles of liberation from sexual, racial, political, religious, economic and class divisions. We exist and communicate on many levels simultaneously, and the flow of our existence energizes us to move beyond the temptations to become paralyzed by inevitable mistakes or to settle for partial solutions.

We are woman lovers, man lovers, self lovers. We exult that our bodies and minds are not taboo to us. We have a revolutionary madness. Our conjectures conjure up the present, for we are witches, we are androgynes, we are monsters. We are you.

Chapter 18

the new human

Jean Rostand

A strange biped that will combine the properties of self-reproduction without males, like the greenfly; of fertilizing his female at long distances like the nautiloid mollusc; of changing sex like the xiphophores; of growing from cuttings like the earthworm; of replacing missing parts like the newt; of developing outside its mother's body like the kangaroo, and of hibernating like the hedgehog.

the contributors

Linda L. Barufaldi is a graduate of the Harvard Divinity School and co-founder of WITCH, Women's Inspirational Theology Conspiracy from Harvard. Her prime interest has been women's liberation and androgyny.

Jeanne Binstock is assistant professor of sociology at the University of Massachusetts in Boston and a specialist in the sociology of the family.

Sidney Callahan has combined several careers as mother of five children, nationally known lecturer, syndicated columnist, and author of *The Illusion of Eve, Working Mother,* and *Parenting: Principles and Politics of Parenthood.*

Alexander Comfort, M.D., Ph.D., is a distinguished and internationally renowned expert in geriatrics and human sexuality. Editor of the best seller *The Joy of Sex* and author of many other books, he is an Associate Fellow of the Center for the Study of Democratic Institutions, director of the Aging Research Institute and professor of zoology at the University College, London.

Emily E. Culpepper is a graduate of the Harvard Divinity School, cofounder of WITCH, Women's Inspirational Theology Conspiracy from Harvard, and a specialist in androgyny and women's liberation.

Leo Davids, assistant professor of sociology at York University, Ontario, Canada, is also an active futurist, specializing in the structure and interactions of parenthood.

Anna K. Francoeur has had a varied career, teaching social studies and mathematics in high schools and comparative civilizations on the college level. With a Master's degree in history from New York University, she is presently a cost accountant with Rowe International, a member of the select Groves Conference on Marriage and the Family, mother of two daughters, and coauthor of *Hot and Cool Sex: Cultures in Conflict* (1974).

George L. Ginsberg, M.D. is associate director of psychiatric services and psychiatrist-in-charge at the New York University Hospital. William A. Frosch and Theodore Shapiro, the coauthors of "The New Impotence," are physician colleagues of Dr. Ginsberg at the New York University Hospital.

Carolyn Heilbrun graduated from Wellesley College and received her Ph.D. from Columbia University, where she is now a professor of English Literature. Along with many articles and reviews, she has published two studies of literary figures, the Garnett family and Christopher Isherwood. Living in New York City with her husband and three children, she most recently authored a full-length study, *Toward a Recognition of Androgyny.*

Raymond J. Lawrence is an Episcopal priest and teaching chaplain at St. Luke's Episcopal Hospital in the Texas Medical Center, Houston. Married for thirteen years, with three children, he also maintains a large marriage counseling practice. His valuable insights into open marriage and satellite relations appear in other publications, notably two essays in Robert H. Rimmer's recent *Adventures in Loving.*

George B. Leonard, for seventeen years a senior editor for *Look* magazine, has also served as vice-president of the Esalen Institute. He is the author of the seminal best seller *Education and Ecstasy, The Man and Woman Thing and Other Provocations,* and *The Transformation: A Guide to the Inevitable Changes in Humankind.*

Elaine Louie is an editor for *Art Direction* and a free-lance writer who has written several essays on the sexual relations and behavior of young people.

Roger W. McIntire has studied, practiced, and taught behavior modification for over a decade. Professor of psychology at the University of Maryland, he is a leading figure in the field of parent training, and has designed behavior-modification programs for the mentally retarded, elementary school children and state programs.

Marshall McLuhan, one of this century's most provocative and controversial thinkers, is director of the Center for Culture and Technology, at the University of Toronto. He is the author of *The Mechanical Bride, The Gutenberg Galaxy, Understanding Media,* and *The Medium Is the Massage.*

Dotson Rader is the editor of *Defiance: A Radical Review* and the author of *I Ain't Marchin' Anymore.* His articles have appeared in *Esquire, Harper's Bazaar,* and *The New York Times.*

Jean Rostand, renowned French embryologist, pioneered the concern over the social consequences of our reproductive technologies with his 1959 book, *Can Man Be Modified?*

Rosemary Radford Reuther, one of America's leading female theologians, is the author of *Liberation Theology* and *The Radical Kingdom,* a contributing editor of *Christianity and Crisis,* the Chauncey Stillman Professor of Roman Catholic Studies at the Harvard University Divinity School (1972–73), and for the past several years professor of historical theology at Howard University.

a selected bibliography

Bartell, G. D. *Group Sex.* New York: Wyden, 1971.

Bernard, J. *The Future of Marriage.* New York: Macmillan, 1971.

Campbell, R. F. "Sex as an intimate communicative act in the decades ahead." *Journal of Home Economics,* November, 1970.

Comfort, A. *The Joy of Sex.* New York: Crown, 1973.

————. *Sex in Society.* New York: Citadel, 1966.

Constantine, L. L., and J. M. Constantine. *Group Marriage.* New York: Macmillan, 1973.

Firestone, S. *The Dialectics of Sex.* New York: William Morrow, 1970.

Ford, C. S., and F. A. Beach. *Patterns of Sexual Behavior.* New York: Harper & Row, 1951.

Francoeur, R. T. *Eve's New Rib: Twenty Faces of Sex, Marriage and Family.* New York: Harcourt Brace Jovanovich/Dell, 1972.

————. *Evolving World, Converging Man.* New York: Holt, Rinehart & Winston, 1970.

————. *Utopian Motherhood: New Trends in Human Reproduction.* New York: Doubleday, 1970; Cranbury, N.J.: A. S. Barnes, 1972.

Francoeur, A. K., and R. T. Francouer. *Hot and Cool Sex: Cultures in Conflict.* New York: Harcourt Brace Jovanovich, 1974.

Heilbrun, C. G. *Toward a Recognition of Androgyny.* New York: Knopf, 1973.

Heinlein, R. *Stranger in a Strange Land.* New York: Berkley, 1961.

Hunt, M. *The Affair.* New York: New American Library, 1969.

————. *The Natural History of Love.* New York: Knopf, 1959.

Janeway, E. *Man's World, Woman's Place.* New York: William Morrow, 1971.

Kirkendall, L. A., and R. N. Whitehurst, ed. *The New Sexual Revolution.* New York: D. Brown, 1971.

Leonard, G. B. *The Transformation: A Guide to the Inevitable Changes in Humankind.* New York: Delacorte, 1972.

Lewinsohn, R. *A History of Sexual Customs.* New York: Harper & Row (Perennial), 1971.

Libby, R. W., and R. N. Whitehurst, eds. *Renovating Marriage: Toward New Sexual Life-Styles.* Danville, Calif.: Consensus, 1973.

Morrison, E. S., and V. Borosage, eds. *Human Sexuality: Contemporary Perspectives.* Palo Alto, Calif.: National Press Books, 1973.

Neubeck, G., ed. *Extramarital Relations*. Englewood Cliffs, N.J.: Prentice-Hall, 1969.

Nobile, P. "What is the New Impotence and Who's Got It?" *Esquire* Magazine, October, 1972.

O'Neill, N., and G. O'Neill. "Is your marriage changing more than you realize?" *Family Circle*, January, 1973.

————. *Open Marriage*. New York: Lippincott, 1972.

Otto, H. A., ed. *The Family in Search of a Future: Alternate Models for Moderns*. New York: Appleton-Century-Crofts, 1970.

Peterman, D. J. "Towards interpersonal fulfillment in an eupsychian culture," *Journal of Humanistic Psychology*, Spring 1972.

Rimmer, R. H. *Adventures in Loving*. New York: New American Library (Signet), 1973.

————. *The Harrad Experiment*. New York: Bantam, 1966.

————. *The Harrad Letters*. New York: New American Library (Signet), 1969.

————. *Proposition 31*. New York: New American Library (Signet), 1968.

————. *The Rebellion of Yale Marratt*. New York: Avon, 1967.

————. *Thursday, My Love*. New York: New American Library (Signet), 1972.

————. *You and I . . . Searching for Tomorrow*. New York: New American Library (Signet), 1971.

Sexuality and the Human Community. Philadelphia: United Presbyterian Church in the U.S.A., 1970.

Richardson, H. W. *Nun, Witch, Playmate: The Americanization of Sex*. New York: Harper & Row, 1971.

Rogers, C. R. *Becoming Partners: Marriage and Its Alternatives*. New York: Delacorte, 1972.

Roszak, B., and T. Roszak, eds. *Masculine/Feminine: Readings in Sexual Mythology and the Liberation of Women*. New York: Harper & Row, 1969.

Roy, R., and D. Roy. *Honest Sex*. New York: New American Library (Signet), 1968.

Sorensen, R. C. *Adolescent Sexuality in Contemporary America. Personal Values and Sexual Behavior, Ages Thirteen to Nineteen*. New York: World, 1973.

Taylor, G. R. *Rethink: A Paraprimitive Solution*. New York: Dutton, 1973.

————. *Sex in History*. London: Thames & Hudson, 1954.

Tofler, A. *Future Shock*. New York: Random House, 1970.